Errata

p. 28   Note no. 16 should
        be deleted

pp. 29-35   Notes 17-26 should
        be renumbered 16-25

p. 35, l. 16 Note no. 26 should
        be inserted after
        the words
        "libertarian free
will),".

LAWLESS MIND

LAWLESS MIND

Raziel Abelson

Temple University Press Philadelphia

Temple University Press, Philadelphia 19122

Copyright © 1988 by Temple University. All rights reserved

Published 1988

Printed in the United States of America

The paper used in this publication meets the minimum
requirements of American National Standard for Information
Sciences—Permanence of Paper for Printed Library Materials,
ANSI Z39.48-1984

Abelson, Raziel.

   Lawless mind / Raziel Abelson.

      p.   cm.

   Bibliography: p.

   Includes index.

   ISBN 0-87722579-6 : $24.95

   1. Mechanism (Philosophy) 2. Mind and body. 3. Man. I. Title.

BD435.A23 1988   88-12358

146'.6—dc19   CIP

To my three outlaws,
GABRIEL, MARIS, and BENJAMIN

Everything is what it is
and not another thing.

—Bishop Joseph Butler

CONTENTS

ix

Contents

Contents

PREFACE

Science and technology are the greatest achievements of western civilization, but they have not been an unmixed blessing, as one is vividly reminded when driving out of New York City during the evening rush hour. Some of the most dramatic breakthroughs of the modern age threaten us with possibly catastrophic side effects. Vast improvements in heating, refrigeration, sewage, and transportation have brought with them life-threatening pollution of air and water. Biomedical advances have increased longevity but have also produced overpopulation and an alarming drain on public resources. Mass media and rapid communication have made possible totalitarian control over large populations. Nuclear energy has created the dangers of core meltdown and thermonuclear holocaust. Developments in molecular biology such as genetic engineering may produce new and uncontrollable microorganisms. But all these dangers, serious though they are, can, one may hope, be kept under control by the very scientific and technological procedures that engendered them. What is not so easily controlled by science itself is the philosophical vision of the world distinctive of the modern age, which science and technology have inspired. It is the mechanistic vision of things that seems to me to pose the greatest danger of all, threatening not our bodily survival but our spiritual well being.

Western civilization engendered science and philosophy, out of which emerged three cosmic visions that characterize its three main epochs: ancient, medieval, and modern. The ancient Greek vision of the world articulated by Plato and Aristotle was organicist and animistic. All things, said Thales, are full of souls, that is, alive. All things pursue their inborn purposes, and man himself is directed by an innate striving toward an ideal state of rationality. The universe was envisioned as an organic unity (in the *Timaeus,* Plato describes it as an animal), every part of which contributes to its overall goal of stability, and the appropriate mode of explanation of recurrent processes is in terms of how they fulfill the innate strivings or final causes of things.

With the rise of Christianity in the late Roman empire, this biological vision of the world was modified into a theological vision, in which the natural teleological order was subordinated to a higher, supernatural order expressive of divine will, and natural processes were considered to be vehicles of divine purpose. In the organicist view of the Greeks, man was considered at home in the world, one particularly complex species among many. In the medieval view, man became partly distinct from nature, with one foot on earth but the other foot in heaven, the bridge between God and nature, sharing features of both.

With the birth of modern science in the seventeenth century, purposive explanation in terms either of innate strivings or of divine will was dispensed with in favor of mechanistic explanation of defining things in terms of measurable ("primary") properties linked by mathematical laws. Anything so explained could be considered a mechanism, that is, a causally determined system such that its state at any one time determines its state at any later time. The vision of all things as mechanistic systems began to dominate western thought. The possibility of this development (already prepared for by the early atomists) was foreseen and deplored by Plato. In the *Phaedo* Socrates notes the difference between purposive and mechanistic explanation:

As if someone, in trying to account for my several actions, said first that the reason why I am lying here now is that my body is composed of bones and sinews, and that the bones are rigid and separated at the joints, but the sinews are capable of contraction and relaxation . . . and since the bones move freely in their joints, the sinews, by relaxing and contracting, enable me to bend my limbs, and that is the cause of my sitting here in a bent position. . . . and never troubled to mention the real reasons, which are that Athens has thought it better to condemn me, therefore I, for my part, have thought it better to sit here. . . .

If it were said that without such bones and sinews and all the rest of them I should not be able to do what I think is right, it would be true. But to say that it is because of them that I do what I am doing, and not through choice of what is best—although my actions are controlled by mind—would be a very lax and inaccurate form of expression.[1]

While the ancient Greeks envisioned the world as a single organism, and the medievals saw it as a kind of stage on which the creations of God act out their assigned roles, modern thought envisions the world as a mechanism composed of smaller mechanisms, down to but perhaps not including subatomic particles. On the ancient view, man is one particularly noble suborganism among others; on the medieval view man is a servant of God, while on the modern view he is a tiny cog in the world machine whose conduct is governed, not ultimately by his own decisions nor by those of God, but by whatever antecedent conditions surround and infuse him, together with the laws of nature. Most philosophers have welcomed the change from the medieval vision to the modern as an Enlightenment and no doubt it is, in many ways. The ancient and medieval views were naively anthropocentric, projecting human purposes first into the rest of nature and then beyond nature. Prediction and control of natural processes became reliable only with the advent of mechanistic explanation and the elimination of purposes and values from the language of science, as Galileo's *Dialogues on Two World Systems* correctly prophesied. The only trouble is that, inspired by the success of the natural sciences, we tend to universalize their mechanistic mode of explanation and then we throw out the humanistic baby with the animistic bathwater, by turning mechanistic explanation backward to explain man himself as just another mechanism, so that his purposes and ideals become superfluous epiphenomena, as Socrates forewarned in the passage cited above. Descartes and the German idealists tried to detach the realm of human action from the grip of mechanism but, as Gilbert Ryle aptly described the effort, they succeeded only in duplicating the physical world with a ghostly mirror image of it that Ryle called the "paramechanical theory of mind." The true escape from mechanism does not lie in that direction.

Why is the mechanistic vision dangerous? As applied to nature, it is a considerable improvement over the ancient and medieval visions, although some modern philosophers, most notably Bergson and Whitehead, have urged us to return to the ancient organicist view. But why go back to something inferior rather than forward to something better? "You can't go home again" seems as true of intellectual history as it is of autobiography. The fact that mechanistic explanation makes possible predictive power and control over natural processes is adequate evidence for the soundness of its vision of nature except for human action. It undermines humanistic culture only when it reaches inward to include ourselves as components of the world machine, that is, when, after banishing purpose and value from nature, it goes on to banish them from humanity as well, as

Socrates foresaw.

The application of mechanistic explanation to human action threatens us with a kind of spiritual annihilation, because it undermines our belief in freedom of the will and with it the reality of choice, value, and moral responsibility. Many of our most eminent thinkers devote their efforts to reducing psychology, ethics, and politics to natural science, by subjecting them to mechanistic explanation. The consequences of following their lead would, I think, be disastrous. We would come to see ourselves no longer as unique subjects of experience and as moral agents endowed with the freedom to create our own purposes and values, and we would come to see ourselves (far too many people already do) as replaceable cogs in the world machine whose desires, beliefs, and ideals are as subject to causal control as are the workings of an automobile, a clock, or a computer.

Wittgenstein once asked us to imagine a tribe of slaveowners who perceive their slaves, not as human individuals with feelings, beliefs, and interests, but as useful and replaceable farm tools. This sort of misperception has since been called aspect-blindness. The mechanistic vision encourages us to be aspect-blind to human freedom, creativity, and responsibility by regarding such features as epiphenomenal, reference to which is needed only where knowledge of the underlying mechanisms is unavailable. The impact of this view on psychology, ethics, and politics is such as to replace moral judgment with the search for causal mechanisms. In psychology it results in reducing moral wisdom to medical therapy, in politics it reduces statesmanship to game theory and rational persuasion to behavioral modification, and in ethics it reduces moral responsibility to social conformity. If we are all programmed automata, as mechanism suggests, then the way to improve our performances is to hire a mechanic of the mind to tinker with our wiring. Is this the way to think about ourselves? I shall try to show that it is not.

I do not presume to offer a new vision of man's place in nature as an alternative to the classical visions that I have found faulty. Wittgenstein held that good philosophy should be limited to exposing bad philosophy, which in turn consists in overextending an initially useful analogy or picture. So perhaps no overall picture can serve us well, and philosophy in the grand style has come to an end. The best I can do is to suggest, in place of the unfolding organism, the actor on the theological stage, the cog in the cosmic machine, and the Cartesian ghost in the bodily machine, the image of a driver of a car who must shift the gears and step on the accelerator to connect causally the motor with the transmission, in order to get anywhere. The mind, let us say, is the motor; the body is the chassis. The obvious flaw in this analogy is that driver, motor, and chassis of any real car are separate entities, unlike person, mind, and body. So we must modify this picture to reveal a car that drives itself. That looks suspiciously like an automaton, but there is this crucial difference: The human vehicle, unlike the mechanical vehicle, decides where and when to go, and could have done otherwise. In brief, picture an animate car, something like the horror-fiction writer Stephen King's murderous automobile, Christine, who runs over everyone in sight, with the proviso that, aside from an occasional Hitler, Charles Manson, or Ayatollah Khomeini, persons are not as malevolent.

Of course, this "vision" is absurdly circular. I have compared a person to a machine that has been personified by comparison to a person. But I am not seriously suggesting that Stephen King ranks with Aristotle, Aquinas, Galileo, and Descartes as the architect of a cosmic vision. I am only illustrating the folly of any kind of reductionism that pretends to explain man by analogy to machines, and, at the same time, I am suggesting that envisioning machines as inanimate persons is no more, and perhaps less, absurd than envisioning persons as animate machines. I have already confessed that I have no new picture to offer that improves on our folk awareness that people have both minds and bodies, and that they have considerable voluntary control over both.

Speaking of faulty pictures, I finished a draft of this study several years ago, but I was very dissatisfied with it because I felt that no clear picture had emerged, so I put it aside until recently. It was rescued from premature burial by Jane Cullen of Temple University Press, who encouraged me to rework it and submit it for publication. Whoever likes what follows has Ms. Cullen to thank.

I would also like to thank L. Jonathan Cohen of Oxford, and my colleagues at N.Y.U., John Carroll, Thomas Nagel, John Richardson, William Ruddick, Roy Sorenson, and Benjamin Zipurski, for their helpful criticisms, and Ulrike Abelson and Deborah Bula for their kind assistance with the manuscript.

Chapter 5 is a revised version of an article, "Psychotherapy and Personal Dignity," published in *Psychoanalysis and Contemporary Thought*, 1978.

Chapter 6 is a revised version of an article, "The Myth of Mental Science," published in B. and E. Bandman, eds., *Bioethics and Human Rights* (Boston: Little Brown, 1978).

Chapter 8 is a revised version of an article, "Does Social Science Provide Causal Explanations?" published in Richard Fox, ed., *Philosophy in Context* (Cleveland: Cleveland State University, 1977).

LAWLESS MIND

1

TWO CONCEPTS OF CAUSE

Causing to Do and Plain Causing

"Cause" is a deep word, a philosophical word. Like other deep, philosophical words such as "reality," "existence," "knowledge," "freedom," and "value," it does a lot of good but occasionally some harm. I want to discuss the harm it does, which, if only occasional, is, I think, so serious on those occasions that, were it the ineluctable price of the good uses, we might do well to heed the advice of Bertrand Russell to dispense with the word once and for all. But I hasten to add that I do not think so high a price need be paid. On the contrary, I hope in this study to show that the occasionally harmful uses of "cause" can be, if not avoided altogether, at least defused of their potential to mislead.

Like all deep philosophical words, "cause" is ambiguous. But that in itself is no great problem. We can deal with ambiguity, systematic or otherwise, by careful attention to context. "Cause" can be used to mean sufficient condition, or necessary condition, or both, or neither. It can be applied to objects, events, states, dispositions, or actions. It can imply necessary connection, or statistical association, or something in between. And the elasticity of the concept can itself "cause" trouble when we draw conclusions from one use that follow only from a different use. Unfortunately this often happens, and then the bad philosophy hits the fan.

These matters have been thoroughly explored by others and I shall not dwell on them. Rather than try to set down rules for how we should and should not use the word, I shall take it as a fact of life that any old thing can be said to be the cause of any other old thing. But in the pages that follow, I hope to show that when we talk about the causes of mental states and voluntary actions our talk should not be taken to have the same implications as when we ascribe causal relations to natural events.

At a diplomatic reception given by an American official, the hostess makes a remark about the high rate of alcoholism in the Soviet Union and the Russian ambassador leaves in a huff. The newspapers then report that the remark of the official's wife caused the ambassador to leave. The slighting remark was the cause; the departure was the effect. Compare this to the following: The overload on the electric circuit caused the fuse to melt. The overload was the cause; the melting of the fuse the effect. These two causal explanations look structurally alike. One might even be tempted, if one were a reporter inclined toward purple prose, to describe the first scenario in language borrowed from the second: The official's wife's remark was too much for the Russian ambassador to bear, causing him to blow his fuse. But consider the differences:

In the first scenario, two voluntary actions are connected by a causal relation, while, in the second, two natural events are so connected. It may be held that voluntary actions are a species of natural events. This much seems obvious: they surely involve natural events. When the official's wife makes her fateful remark, an event occurs consisting in her utterance, and when the ambassador leaves, an event occurs consisting in his departure. But whether a voluntary action just is (nothing but) an event in the world seems less obvious.

Wittgenstein asked what remains when we subtract the event of one's arm rising from the action of raising one's arm.[1] It is hard to imagine any more correct answer than: Nothing. And yet raising one's arm is surely not just the event of one's arm rising, since the latter need not be voluntary. Wittgenstein's point was, presumably, that a voluntary action is not a complex of which the bodily movement and the intention are two distinct component events, in the way that the storming of the city and the slaughtering of the inhabitants are component events that together made up the destruction of Troy. If this was Wittgenstein's point he was surely right, since one could intend to raise one's arm and it could rise due to a neural spasm, yet one would not thereby have performed the voluntary action of raising one's arm. That action cannot then be a mere conjunction of two simpler events consisting in the internal or mental event of intending to raise one's arm and the observable physical event of one's arm rising. What seems to be missing is the because relation, that one's arm rises *because* one intends it to do so, a relation that persuades dualists to hold that the intention is a mental event that causes a bodily movement, and persuades materialists to hold that an intention is identical to some unknown physical event occurring in the brain. But neither account can be right. If the relation between the intention and the bodily movement were a causal relation between two distinct events, whether mental or physical, then they would occur either simultaneously or sequentially. If sequentially, then the intention was not the unconditional intention to raise one's arm now, but the conditional intention to raise one's arm at some later moment provided that the reason for doing so remains operative. If simultaneously, then in the normal circumstance that the agent is not prevented from carrying out his or her intention, there is no way to distinguish the two alleged events: to intend to do something just is to do it intentionally. Thus considering an intention to act as a mental event distinct from the act intended fails to satisfy the Humean condition of independent identifiability, no mater how liberally the causal relation is understood, that is, no matter how wide the categorial range employed, and no matter how weak the criteria of its application.

Consider some of the differences between intentional actions and natural events that are not captured by assimilating our earlier example of the hostess and the ambassador to the Humean causal relation between natural events:

1. The relation between the remark of the hostess and what the ambassador then did depended obviously on what the ambassador understood to be the intended meaning of the remark, the attitude motivating it, and the degree to which the hostess' attitude was shared by other Americans, as well as on what he believed to be the appropriate diplomatic response to the expression of such an attitude. The alleged causal relation between the two actions is thus mediated by various mental processes of interpretation, inference, judgment, and decision. The deceptively simple logical form of one action causing another to occur disguises or at least abbreviates a very complex structure. In contrast, the overload causing the melting of the fuse is a direct relation between the two events, such that nothing has to be known about mediating internal processes as constituting that causal relation. This is quite apart from the fact that asserting a causal relation presupposes all sorts of standard necessary conditions. That is equally true of both scenarios.

2. I have commented elsewhere on the importance of the difference of meaning between plain causing and causing to do. Causing an agent to perform a voluntary action is a generic notion whose species are persuading, inciting, influencing, coercing, bribing, seducing, cajoling, and so on, while plain causing is not at all agenus of distinct species of activities, indeed, it is not any kind

of activity, but simply a relation between events. "How did X cause Y to do A?" calls for an account of the values, beliefs, aims, and habits of X and Y, while "How did C cause E?" calls only for initial conditions. The first question is psychological; the second is not.

3. A third difference is that an agent can be caused to do something independently of the real existence of the cause. Agents notoriously react to what they take to be the case whether or not it really is the case, and their responses to what is not the case can be said to be caused by such non-entities or non- facts just as truly as it can be said to be caused by something real. This may be the reason why we are often tempted to regard inaction as if it too were an event endowed with causal powers. For example, my daughter's failure to come to the dinner table when I call her "causes" me to raise my voice. Man, says Sartre, is the only being who can respond to what does not exist. His claim seems a bit anthropocentric considering that animals too can misread intentions and react to imaginary dangers or delights, like the dog in Aesop's fable who loses his bone while snapping at the reflection in the river. In any event, it is an odd kind of cause that can bring about its effect even when it does not exist.[2]

4. Perhaps the most important difference (which also explains difference 2 above) is the apparently triadic character of causing to do, as contrasted with the dyadic character of plain causing. If we are to manage with one concept of cause, then the triadic relation should turn out to be a complex conjunction of dyadic relations, which is what deterministic-minded philosophers suggest. On the other hand, its irreducible triadicity would seem to be a necessary condition for ascribing moral responsibility for an action, for if the agent is not essentially involved in the causal nexus, then how can it be said to be his or her action? So the issue of whether causing to do

is triadic or dyadic would seem to lie at the core of the free will controversy.

Dyadic reductions of causing to do locate the dyadic relation inside the agent, either in his brain or in his mind, thus making the agent's brain or mind a battleground and the agent himself a victim or beneficiary of the outcome of the battle. Donald Davidson and Alvin Goldman, among others, locate the causal relation as holding between the agent's primary reason and the appropriate bodily movement. Wilfrid Sellars, John Searle, and Myles Brand locate it between intention and bodily movement. Both positions have their difficulties, as we shall see in detail later on. Their common problem will be explaining why the agent is responsible for a relation in which he plays no active part.

It looks as if either reasons are not causes, and voluntary actions are not causally explainable, or else the causal connection is mediated by the agent's decision and, without that decision, is non-necessitating. In my earlier book, *Persons,* I took the former line. I now propose to take the latter line. There is no incompatibility between these two lines of thought; indeed, the difference is, I think, purely terminological. For even if reasons are granted causal efficacy, they still depend, for their efficacy, on the decision of the agent and therefore cannot be considered to be causes that necessitate their effects or, if all actual causes necessitate, they are merely potential, not actual, causes.

Does this mean that there are two kinds of causality at work, the one (physical) a dyadic relation between events linked by a causal law, and the other (psychological) a triadic relation between a reason or motive, an agent, and a thought or action, such that there is no law by which the motivation C necessitates the thought or action E?[3] If the causal link in psychological causality is not one of necessitation, then what is its character? It has sometimes been suggested (e.g., by Carl Hempel) that C makes E more probable. But that won't do because making probable is still a dyadic relation between two events or classes of events and leaves out the essential third term, the agent. C might very well make E more probable for one agent but not for another. Shall we say then that E itself already includes reference to a particular agent, being not just the abstract doing of something, but A's doing of that thing? In such case there is surely no law, whether uniform or statistical, that connects cause with effect, unless the agent A is reducible to some set of impersonal conditions. (We will later consider the soundness of this latter proposal, which has been made by Derek Parfit.)

Trigger Events

Another way of looking at the problem is this: The total antecedent condition that necessitates an effect consists of a set of background conditions or dispositional properties plus a trigger event that actualizes the relevant dispositions; for example, immersion in a liquid actualizes or triggers the dissolution potential (solubility) of a solid. What could be the trigger event that actualizes the psychological dispositions (character traits, emotions, and desires) of an agent so that he performs a voluntary action? Let us say, following Davidson, that a voluntary action is caused by the agent's primary reason, consisting of the agent's desire for something and her belief that the action in question is the best way to satisfy the desire. Beliefs and desires, as usually understood, are dispositional properties, which may hold of the agent even when he or she is not performing the action in question. Some trigger event is needed to actualize the relevant dispositions, for example, the whiff of freshly baked bread that sends me rushing into the bakery. Then, given the appropriate desires and beliefs as background conditions, my olfactory experience S triggers the response E of rushing into the bakery. But still, there is something missing from this picture, namely, me. Presumably S triggers *my* response E, but not yours, if you don't particularly care for fresh bread.

I may desire fresh bread, smell the aroma, and nevertheless decide that I don't have time to stop en route to an appointment, or that I had better forego the extra calories for the sake of my waistline. In brief, other desires may countervail this one. But then, what trigger event determines which desire prevails? If I am an incurable fresh bread consumer, although the aroma in a statistical sense makes my purchase more probable, my actual decision may well be to pass it by, in which case the olfactory stimulus S can hardly be said to cause a response E that does not in fact occur. What then would explain the decision to refrain from buying the bread? Is the trigger event, in such case, my decision to forego the pleasure for the sake of duty or prudence? Is a decision a trigger event? If so, what would be the trigger event that brought about the decision? Presumably, since we are considering voluntary action, for which the agent's decision is a necessary condition, that trigger event would be a second-order decision to make the relevant first-order decision to forebear from purchasing the bread, for if the process leading to the first-order decision was not within my power to decide, then neither was its effect, my action, and in that case, my action was not voluntary, contrary to our hypothesis. Thus looking for higher-order causes of lower-order decision leads us into vicious regress that Gilbert Ryle warns about with respect to alleged acts of volition, or else disqualifies decisions for the role of trigger events.

There is a further reason why decisions cannot qualify as trigger events. One's decision to perform an action A may or may not be simultaneous with performing A.[4] If it is, then it is not a separate event, but a feature of A itself, namely the feature of being voluntary, intentional, purposeful, or deliberate. If, on the other hand, the decision was arrived at prior to the action, then it was only a provisional decision, subject to cancellation or reaffirmation. In such case, it is clearly not the trigger event we were looking for, but only an additional disposition or background condition that still requires an activating trigger.

Having argued that decisions cannot qualify as trigger events that activate the dispositions we have called "primary reasons," because so considering them would detach decisions from their authors, or else engender an infinite regress of higher-order decisions, I conclude that psychological causality is irreducibly triadic and indeterministic. It is not analyzable into two dyadic causal relations, one between stimulus and decision and another between decision and action, because decisions cannot play this mediating role of trigger events, and it is indeterministic because the causal relation between primary reason and action requires the agent's decision, which is not determined by antecedent causes. To say that the agent could have decided otherwise is to say that the primary reason that was the cause of the action would not have caused it, had the agent not decided to perform the action.

2

AGENCY AND RESPONSIBILITY

Persons as Agents

What sort of thing is an agent, the nub of the triadic relation of psychological causality, who mediates between reason-cause and action-effect by deciding to act on a reason? The paradigm of agency is the normal human adult person. It is from Mommy and Daddy or their surrogates that, early in life, we form the concept of agency and acquire some skill at psychological understanding of ourselves and others. What about animals, corporations, nations, robots, ghosts, or deities? Are they agents too? Is everything an agent, including the entire universe, as the ancient Greek hylozoists believed, or, on the other hand, is nothing really an agent, as mechanists seem to tell us? Let's start with our paradigms, and go on from there.

What is a normal adult human person? Is it an enduring, unchanging entity, conforming to the classical notion of a substance, as some philosophers, such as Joseph Butler, Thomas Reid, and Roderick Chisholm, have maintained,[1] or is it a sequence of transient phenomena, such as Hume's bundles of experiences (recently revived by David Lewis and Derek Parfit),[2] entities that are themselves reducible to non-personal constituents, such as causal relations between stimuli and responses for Lewis, or relations of connected-ness and continuity between subsequent experiences and an initial set for Parfit? If a person is an enduring, unchanging substance, must he or she be a Cartesian *res cogitans*? Some people believe there are subagents, brain modules, for example, or Freud's ego, super-ego, and id, and some people believe there are superagents, such as social groups, classes, nations, God, and the universe. Are these extended concepts of agency helpful? I think not, for the following reason:

A person is a creature who can tell you what he or she is doing and experiencing. Entities that cannot do so may be considered quasi-persons by extension insofar as they might, under imaginable cir-cumstances, be able to do so, for example, toddlers and animals, if they had the gift of language, or lunatics and comatose patients, if they were restored to normalcy. But since this ground does not apply to either subpersons or superpersons, they seem to me to be dispensable extravagances. Parfit argues that ordinary persons are equally dispensable, but he arrives at this conclusion only by under-estimating the importance of cognitive authority and moral respon-sibility. Brain modules, social classes, nations, corporations, and robots cannot tell us with personal authority what they are experi-encing and doing, nor can they be punished or rewarded for their actions, except by punishing or rewarding their members or (in the case of robots) their operators. Reductionists like Parfit suggest that cognitive authority and moral responsibility are themselves dispens-able extravagances, even where ordinary persons are concerned. But they have a heavy burden of proof in this regard. For the reasons why they cannot successfully carry that burden, I refer the reader to P. F. Strawson's essay "Freedom and Resentment."[3] For my part, I would add that, if these data for an adequate theory of mind are to be brushed aside, then it is hard to see just what data remain to be explained.

We need not concern ourselves here with the classical problem of personal identity over time, that is, in virtue of what facts we can know that this person now is the same as the person then. We may take bodily continuity as the criterion of third-person identity, and memory as the criterion of self-identity over time. Knotty problems remain about what to do when these standard criteria fail to coincide, but they need not concern us here. What concerns us here is the nature of the nub of the triadic causal process: reason-agent-action, that is, what it is that makes an action the voluntary action of an agent or (in standard cases) a person.

The materialist answer of D. M. Armstrong and others is that voluntary action essentially involves the agent's body, especially the nervous system, is a normal sort of way that excludes seizures and compulsions. But how identify that "normal sort of way" except to say that only those actions that the agent can authoritatively report *and for which she can be held fully responsible* are distinctively her own? So if we brush aside as superfluities the features of cognitive authority and moral responsibility, there is no longer any *point* to distinguishing voluntary actions from seizures, or, for that matter, psychological from physical causality.

What makes an action the agent's action is what one has some control over, that is, what one can decide, in two senses of "decide": (1) one decides one's actions (and experiences) in having the cognitive authority to say, without fear of contradiction, what one perceives, feels, believes, and is doing, and (2) one decides one's actions in providing the causal link between motivating reason and appropriate bodily movement. This would seem to be the intimate sense of ownership that enables us to distinguish one's own experience or action from one's own sneeze.

Let us consider more closely the relation between the concept of a person or paradigm agent and that of moral responsibility. A person is a creature that has rights, authority, and responsibility, three features that go naturally together. To carry out one's responsibilities, one must have the cognitive and volitional authority to make the necessary decisions. Moreover, there is little point to having authority to make decisions if one doesn't have the right to employ the necessary means of carrying them out; thus a responsible agent must have certain fundamental (in H. L. A. Hart's sense, "natural") rights constituting social recognition of his or her cognitive and volitional authority, such as the right to be believed, to have his or her interests considered as reasons for action, and to be unhindered in the pursuit of those interests. In turn, the agent's assumption of cognitive and volitional authority commit him or her to respect the equal authority of others and to accept responsibility for actions affecting their interests. Authority and responsibility seem natural correlates that vary together. The more one gains or lacks of the one, the more one gains or lacks of the other. Thus animals, infants, madmen, and idiots have minimal authority and minimal responsibility, while heads of state and heads of families have maximum degrees of both.

These social facts and conceptual relations should be kept in mind when formulating metaphysical theories directed toward solving problems like personal identity over time, mind-body interaction, and free will. Any theory that entails the denial of these facts, for example, the denial that people really have moral responsibilities or cognitive authority, would have to have an awful lot going for it in other respects to compensate for its patent inadequacy in this regard. This consideration leads us into the issue of the compatibility of free will with causal determinism.

Two Conditions of Responsibility: Voluntariness and Rationality

If, as I have claimed, authority and responsibility are the essential features of agency, and thus of person-status, then a theory of mind will have to account for these features above all. Yet surprisingly, most theorists of mind have neglected to do so. For example, David Armstrong's otherwise impressive work, *A Materialist Theory of Mind*,[4] does not even discuss responsibility. In arguing for a central-state theory of mind and against dualism, idealism, parallelism, and attribute emergentism, Armstrong persuasively maintains that his theory has more explanatory power than any of these rivals, but among the important phenomena to be explained, such as causal interaction between mind and body, intentionality, and disembodied existence, he does not include moral responsibility. His two chapters (8 and 9) on the will explain voluntary action as bodily movement initiated and sustained by a mental cause controlled by informational feedback in such a way as to bring about a desired end-state. At no point in his analysis does he consider the question of whether the purposive structure so described is to be attributed to the agent, or to an external cause. For example, a computerized "smart" missile would satisfy Armstrong's definition of voluntary agency, but the inability of the missile to desist from its activity (for example, if a truce were declared before it reached its target) shows that it is not really the author of its behavior, that is, not a responsible agent.

Some philosophers, dubbed "hard determinists" by William James, dismiss the very concept of moral responsibility as delusory, and so see no need to explain ascriptions of it as other than delusive beliefs due to ignorance of the antecedent causes of action. Spinoza, Paul d' Holbach, and, in recent times, John Hospers, Paul Edwards, J. J. C. Smart, Derek Parfit, and Galen Strawson[5] have taken this line. Does this strategy make sense? What, after all, is a theory of mind or a theory of action supposed to explain? If it need only explain the fact that human behavior is more complex than that of, say, guided missiles, then of course the greater complexity of functioning is adequately explained by a greater complexity of internal structure. But that is too easy a victory. It is one thing to claim, as compatibilists like Daniel Dennett do, that responsibility is definable in terms of complexity of causal structure—which at least acknowledges responsibility as a datum to be accounted for—and quite another to dismiss it as illusory, as hard determinists do. I suspect that a close examination of both views would reveal that they rely on each other at crucial points, compatibilists falling back on the hard determinist denial of the reality of moral responsibility when challenged to identify the subject of responsibility, once the agent has been dissolved into a battleground of causal factors, and hard determinists falling back on the compatibilist redefinition of responsibility when challenged to justify the social practices of blame and punishment.

Two conditions are commonly recognized as necessary for the fair ascription of moral responsibility to an agent: (1) free will or capacity for voluntary action and (2) rationality or capacity for selecting intelligent means to achieve desired ends. The first condition, voluntariness, is the more controversial and is subject to varied interpretation and even to wholesale rejection or dissolution into some aspect of the second condition. These conditions underlie two kinds of excuses: those that nullify, and those that merely reduce to some degree the agent's responsibility for what he or she has done. (The reason for this difference is, I suggest, that rationality is a matter of degree once voluntariness is assumed, while voluntariness is all or nothing.) These two conditions are all too often conflated, as a result of which one of them, usually the second (rationality), is made to bear the weight of both, which, as we shall see, it cannot do without collapsing.

The sole condition for holding agents responsible for their actions, compatibilists maintain, is that the causal antecedents of their actions be of the right type, for example, that they have the informational feedback structure described by Armstrong as a result of which undesireable actions can be deterred by the likelihood of blame or punishment. On this view, holding an agent responsible means threatening him with blame or punishment and the point of doing so is to deter him from doing what he would otherwise be inclined to do. This account explains well enough why we do not nowadays hold lunatics, toddlers, or household pets responsible for their behavior. They simply are not rational enough to be deterred by social threats, and it would be unjustly vindictive to blame or punish creatures when it will in no way benefit anyone to do so. But does this account explain equally well why we do not hold inanimate beings like robots responsible, even when they are capable of performing tasks as well as animate beings and when they exhibit sufficiently complex informational-feedback causal structures? It is not for lack of rationality that a computerized robot cannot be deterred from what it is bent on doing, but for lack of free will or voluntariness. In explaining when we should hold human beings responsible Dennett sensibly acknowledges both conditions, voluntariness and rationality, but, except for an element of randomness that we will shortly consider, he tends to reduce voluntariness to an aspect of rationality and concentrates exclusively on the latter condition. It is all too easy to do so, because ordinarily we simply presuppose voluntariness when we assess degree of rationality in children, animals, and the mentally defective. But what is this voluntariness condition that we presuppose? Mechanists like Dennett who hold that we ourselves are complex robots deprive themselves of any basis for distinguishing these two conditions for responsibility.

Some particularly subtle mechanists, like Searle and Dreyfus, suggest that the difference can be found in the hardware, rather than the software, of the agent. Their view is that only animate creatures equipped with sense organs, glands, and central nervous systems that entertain sensations, desires, emotions, and beliefs are capable of voluntary action. But they leave out the crucial factor that distinguishes free agency from sphexishness (to use Dennett's apt nomenclature), namely, the ability to do otherwise.

Full-Blooded Desires and Tropisms

Let's consider the first condition, voluntariness. Is there really such a thing and, if so, is it consistent with determinism? A good way to approach this question is in terms of the dilemma formulated by A. I. Melden and Thomas Nagel, among others,[6] which I will refer to, for the sake of brevity, as the Melden-Nagel dilemma, or still more briefly, the M-N dilemma, as follows: If, given all the antecedent conditions of action, there is only one possible outcome or (to acknowledge Henry Frankfurt's paradox of the evil scientist controlling an agent's desires and decisions)[7] only one possible decision, then the agent cannot help doing what he does and is not morally responsible for doing it. On the other hand, if his action is not necessitated by the antecedent conditions, including his reasons, then it is an arbitrary, haphazard event that is more aptly described as happening to the agent than as something he voluntarily does, and again he does not appear to be morally responsible for it. After careful investigation of both horns of this dilemma, Nagel despairs of a solution, finding both horns equally unpalatable.[8]

David Wiggins insists (rightly, in my opinion) that there must be an escape between the horns. Most compatibilists cheerfully impale themselves on the determinist horn, insisting that, if it is covered by sufficient padding, it won't hurt. C. A. Campbell, Roderick Chisholm, and others have tried to transcend the dilemma by distinguishing agent causality from event causality,[9] but this maneuver only results in double impalement. On the event level, it means impalement on the haphazard horn; on the agent causality level, the dilemma reappears, as follows: Is the agent's causing of his action necessitated by antecedent conditions or not? If it is, then one can't help it and isn't responsible. If not, then, according to Melden and Nagel, one's causing of one's action is a haphazard event that happens to one and again one is not responsible for it. Introducing the mysterious notion of agent causation accomplishes nothing more than to wrap the mystery in an enigma. Peter van Inwagen, Richard Peters, Anthony Kenny, John Lucas, and a few others have preferred impalement on the indeterminist horn.[10] I propose a less suicidal strategy, that of searching for space between the horns whereby, although the action is explainable by reasons (call them causes, if you like, but not dyadic, determinist causes) and therefore is not haphazard, random, or arbitrary, it was not necessitated by those reasons (at least not in the causal sense of "necessitated"), insofar as the agent could have decided otherwise. A more careful examination of the two conditions for responsibility, voluntariness and rationality, may enable us to find the needed space between the horns of the M-N dilemma.

Animals, said Aristotle, have locomotive souls, meaning that, unlike rocks and plants, they can set themselves in motion. But cannot an inaminate object, of the kind we call an automaton, set itself in motion? Doesn't a furnace equipped with a thermostat and self-starting ignition "turn itself on"? Not really. A fall in the surrounding temperature causes a switch to close, which activates the ignition system. So nothing literally sets itself in motion, but each event is brought about by something external to itself.

But the same could be said to be true of animals, including human beings. When a predatory animal sights its prey, it may appear as if it spontaneously decides to attack, but in reality the sight of its prey causes, in the sense that it triggers, the attack, just as the falling temperature causes the furnace to ignite. What's the difference? The non-mechanist protests that the difference is pretty obvious: the predatory animal wants to capture and eat its prey, while the automatic heating system has no wants at all; it just does what it was designed to do under certain physical conditions. The mechanist can then reply that the predatory animal also just does what it was genetically programmed or conditioned by its experiences to do under certain conditions such as the appearance of its prey. And no matter how rational, intellectual, and spiritual humans are, isn't it plausible to assume that we too are programmed or conditioned to do what we do given the eliciting circumstances, so that, if the furnace doesn't really start itself but is started by the falling temperature, it is equally true that animals don't really set themselves in motion in pursuit of their prey but are set in motion by the visual or olfactory stimulation, and we too don't really make up our own minds, say, to search for the meaning of life in a Tibetan monastery, but are spurred to do so by whatever cultural influences and innate predilections are at work within and around us. And so the ball continues back and forth across the net.

The sophisticated mechanist, for example, Daniel Dennett, intervenes to raise the level of the debate, as follows: Of course there is a profound difference between phenomena like the search for the meaning of life, on the one hand, and, on the other, the auto-ignition of a heating system, but it is a difference of complexity of structure rather than a difference of metaphysical nature (whatever that may mean). The discussion must therefore be deepened to take account of three features that automata do not manifest, but humans and animals do, in order to see whether they are indeed features due merely to complexity of structure, or whether they require a more radical, perhaps even metaphysical, explanation. These features are: (a) desire, (b) means-end reasoning, and (c) self-monitoring. Let's consider them in turn.

Almost anyone agrees that (most) animals have desires. Even Descartes, who considered non-human animals to be unconscious automata, granted them unconscious, purely physiological desires. Whether physiologically determined, unconscious desires, or tropisms, satisfy the full-blooded concept of desire is a matter of dispute among materialists. Eliminative materialists, like Stephen Stich, Myles Brand, and Paul Churchland, regard the concept of desire in its ordinary, "folk-psychological" use as hopelessly incoherent, so that insisting on it as an essential condition of genuine agency invalidates the concept of agency.[11] (The same criticism has been made of the concept of belief, and thus both of Davidson's components of psychological causality have been brought into question.) These writers want to reduce the full concept of desire to the behavioristic concept of tropism such as is exemplified by the inclination of a plant toward the sunlight. The difference, for them, between the desire to find the meaning of life and the heliotropic plant's "desire" for the sunlight is only in degree of complexity; for example, the tropism is, as Ryle put it, "single-track," capable of producing only one kind of response, namely, bending toward the sun, while the full-blooded desire is many-track, producing different behavior under different conditions, both environmental and internal.[12] Functionalists like Dennett and Sayre require a more radical difference, and find it in the order of causality involved. Dennett proposes that a creature genuinely desires an end-state if and only if its tendency to act toward that end-state is guided by its processes of reasoning and self-monitoring. So the full-blooded concept of desire, in contrast to its pale tropistic surrogate, involves internal processes that mediate between external stimuli and overt responses. Are these internal processes all that is involved in agency; is this the nub of triadic causality? If so, the triadic relation dissolves into a dyadic chain of stimulus–data-processing, data-processing–action. But wait, the data-processing includes a special component, for Dennett, namely, a self-representation in relation to which some responses are judged inconsistent and inhibited, while others are approved and reinforced. In brief, the system learns to achieve its desired end-state efficiently, or to abandon it if it is judged incompatible with other desired states. So we do after all retain a third relatum of the causal relation, namely, the self-representation of the system that guides its learning process. But what is it that does the self-representing; is it the entire system or one part of it? If I forebear from satisfying my desire for fresh bread to satisfy my self-image of a slender person, is it I or my self-image that inhibits the desire? When a machine has a self-monitoring module that inhibits a response, it is not really monitoring itself, but rather one part of it is monitoring the rest, like a foreman on an assembly line, whereas in our own case, it is not our self-image module, but we in our entirety, who decide whether or not to satisfy a desire or to suppress it, and it is the capacity for such decisions that distinguishes us from self-monitoring automata.[13]

In any event, desire, to be done full justice, must be recognized to be a very complex state, involving self-monitoring, whether by the whole system or by part of it. The question remains, what sort of thing is the self that monitors itself? If it is just some module of the system, then there is no unified agent, and the casual chain is dyadic. If the latter, then the mere complexity of the process is not enough to justify the claim that the system desires the end-state toward which it acts, even in this more sophisticated sense of desire involving self-monitoring and learning, for it must also be capable of deciding either way—to satisfy its desire or to inhibit it, to act or to forebear. It is not possible to define voluntariness simply as ability to do what one desires to do, as reductive materialists such as Hobbes have often proposed, if we are able to distinguish mere tropism from full-blooded desire. Realizing this, Dennett proposes to make the second and third conditions, reasoning and self-monitoring, modify the first. I don't think this strategy can accomplish its purpose.

Second-Order Decisions and Desires

Dennett grants that mere degree of causal complexity is not enough to distinguish tropistic behavior, or "sphexishness," as he calls it, on analogy to the automatic responses of the sphex wasp, from the voluntary behavior of rational agents. The *type* of causal complexity is, he recognizes, all-important. A capacity for full-blooded desire requires the information-processing and self-monitoring essential to learning, and the latter, in turn, requires self-representation. He thinks both conditions can be satisfied by sophisticated machines, and perhaps he is right. But the question remains whether these features that account for the rationality of conduct also account for its voluntariness or whether, to constitute genuine, full-blooded rationality rather than the pale simulation of rationality, voluntariness must already be presupposed.

Imagine an entity that has no capacity for desire, yet satisfies all the observable conditions for rationality; it selects means toward achieving end-states G (l to n), and it monitors its successes and failures, repeating the former and avoiding repetitions of the latter, for example, a chess-playing computer. But it couldn't care less whether or not it wins. Nevertheless it seems to make every effort to win, and it usually does win. How do we know that it doesn't want to win, that it doesn't have a desire for victory? I think the answer is that we cannot conceive of any non-physical conditions under which it would forebear from trying to win. No one could bribe it or rationally persuade it to make less of an "effort." The antecedent conditions, both hardware and software, necessitate its apparent efforts, which, for that reason, are not full-blooded efforts but mere tropisms that are not motivated by desire. Full-blooded desire is subject to defeat by contrary desires.

Suppose we make the machine simulate conflicts of desires and their resolution in the following way: We program it to aim at alternative end-states, such as (a) winning at chess, (b) solving a differential equation, or (c) detecting enemy aircraft, and it cannot pursue more than one of these at a time. How will it "decide" which end-state to pursue first? One way would be to program it with a lexical ordering of goals, say, first detect enemy aircraft, then solve an equation, and lastly play chess when challenged. A second way, suggested by Dennett, would be to build in a randomizing element like a three-sided die whose toss would make the "decision" a matter of chance. In either case, although, given the initial step of selecting its goal, subsequent moves would satisfy the criteria of rationality, the initial step would not. In the first case it would be causally necessitated by the lexical ordering, while in the second case it would be random. Here is the M-N dilemma all over again.

The trouble is that in neither case has the "desire" to achieve end-state G been overcome by a greater desire to achieve a different and incompatible end-state G'. Why is the lexical ordering of end-states not indicative of relative strength of desires? The answer is, that this ordering was externally imposed on the machine by its programmer. But then what if the machine orders itself lexically in accordance with a more general program that instructs it to sub-program itself with different lexical orderings on different occasions, depending perhaps, on which button is initially depressed by its operator? Will this satisfy the requirement that we be able to distinguish simulated from genuine desire? The answer is no, because such "self"-programming is, in turn, either predetermined or random. Are we any different? Perhaps not. If it were shown that our goals and their relative strengths were either predetermined by genetic programming and cultural conditioning, or else randomly generated, then we would have to conclude that there simply is no such thing as full-blooded desire, and we would have to agree with Stich's critique of folk psychology. The concept of desire would not be shown to be incoherent, but it would be exposed as empirically vacuous, a mere I.O.U., as some writers have suggested, for an as yet unavailable causal explanation, of which preprogramming and random generation are the exhaustive subspecies.

All this is well-traveled territory, and I make no pretense of saying anything new. I wish merely to point out what follows from the second-order determinism described above. If no apparent desires are full-blooded in that the relative strength of action tendencies, whether first order or higher-order, is either predetermined or randomly generated, then the voluntariness condition of free agency has been reduced to an aspect of the rationality condition, that is, to reasoning and self-monitoring. That, indeed, is the sophisticated compatibilist solution to the problem of free will. But is it a genuine solution, or has the question been begged? What remains of the rationality condition itself if full-blooded desire has disappeared, that is, if the allegedly rational agent is not acting to satisfy his or her desires, but is obeying programmed instructions or responding to randomly generated impulses? It would appear that full-blooded rationality goes the way of full-blooded desire, dissolving into a particularly complex structure of tropisms, and we are impaled on either horn of the second-order M-N dilemma.

Full-Blooded Rationality

This conflation of voluntariness with rationality plagues the most subtle and persuasive statement of compatibilism, namely, P. F. Strawson's renowned essay "Freedom and Resentment." Strawson argues as follows: It cannot be the case that determinism, whatever that view is (Strawson professes not to be clear on just what determinism involves), entails that people are never free and responsible, since freedom and responsibility are plain facts of social life, while determinism is some fuzzy metaphysical claim that might be true and might be false—who knows? Attitudes of resentment, admiration, gratitude, contempt, pity, forgiveness, trust, approval, and indignation comprise our relations to each other to so great an extent that social life without them is unimaginable. Thus any philosophical view that advises us to refrain from such attitudes, or at least implies that they are illusions due to ignorance of causes, is advising us to live like robots rather than like human beings. Strawson grants that there are situations in which a more "objective" attitude is appropriate, particularly when dealing with small children or the mentally ill. But normally, our relations to each other involve the morally reactive attitudes that are ruled out by what he calls the "objective attitude."

There is a problem in Strawson's nomenclature. The attitude we take toward small children and the mentally ill or retarded is not as impersonal as Strawson suggests. It would be less misleading to call the attitude of not holding children, lunatics, or idiots responsible for undesireable actions "paternalistic" rather than "objective." For we do not consider such subjects to be mere objects of manipulation. While we may not adopt negative morally reactive attitudes toward them, we may be expected to adopt positive attitudes, for example, to approve and reward them for positive achievements. Our feelings of concern for the naive and the disadvantaged motivate protectiveness and suspension of moral criticism, but not suspension of approval and praise. Strawson should have distinguished this paternalistic attitude from a third, more truly objective attitude that is usually taken toward wild animals, plants, and inanimate objects. This oversight is not minor, but is due to a profound misunderstanding. Strawson wants to argue that those (namely, hard determinists like d'Holbach) who believe that determinism is incompatible with freedom and responsibility (Strawson calls them pessimists) are proposing, in effect, that the paternalistic attitude is always the proper one to take. But the paternalistic attitude is not supported by determinism. Psychiatrists for whom all the world's a couch may urge us to regard everyone except themselves as an infant or a lunatic, but they cannot appeal to determinism as their logical ground. The attitude that is really supported by determinism is the third attitude described above—treating persons as mere objects to be analyzed, manipulated, and sometimes enjoyed, like plants, wild animals, and nature in general.[14] The source of Strawson's mistake in confusing the paternalistic attitude toward immature and defective agents with the impersonal or objective attitude toward non-persons, is that he has conflated the two conditions for moral responsibility: voluntariness and rationality. Infants and lunatics are agents, capable of voluntary, self-initiated activity, but they are not sufficiently rational to be held fully responsible for their actions. Since both conditions are necessary for moral responsibility, they are somewhat immune to blame, resentment, and other expressions of negative morally reactive attitudes, but not to those of positive appreciation. This confusion underlies one of Strawson's most powerful arguments for compatibilism, as follows:

> Would it not be grotesque to think of the development of the child as a progressive or patchy emergence from an area in which its behavior is in this sense determined into an area where it isn't? Whatever sense of "determined" is required in stating the thesis of determinism, it can scarcely be such as to allow of compromise, borderline style answers to the question, "Is this bit of behavior determined or isn't it?"[15]

Strawson's point is that responsibility is a matter of degree. As children mature they become more and more responsible for their actions. Yet whether or not an action was causally determined cannot be a matter of degree. Either it was or it wasn't. So far, he is quite right. But his conclusion, that determinism is irrelevant to moral responsibility, would only follow if the degree of rationality of the agent that serves as the measure of the degree of responsibility were the sole condition relevant to the ascription of responsibility. He here overlooks the fact that the question of the degree of rationality of the agent cannot even arise until the prior question, whether voluntary agency is at work at all, has been answered affirmatively.

Some philosophers insist that there can be rationality without voluntary agency. I have in mind those, like Sayre and Dennett, who ascribe rationality to computers.[16] I have already argued against that conception of rationality, but the matter need not occupy us here, since if we allow rationality to be predicted of machines, that would provide even more reason for distinguishing the rationality condition from the voluntariness condition of responsibility. I don't think Dennett or Sayre wants to reward and punish machines for their accomplishments and misdeeds. It would be silly to scold a chair that has fallen on one's foot, or a car that has failed to start, not because the chair and the car are too immature to know better, but because they are not capable of voluntary action. This is not the reason why it is wrong to resent and blame small children and mental defectives. Children and lunatics are as capable of voluntary action as any paragon of rationality. Rationality is, as Strawson contends, a matter of degree. Children and lunatics have reasons for what they do that are often bad reasons from the standpoint of adult standards of good and bad, and goodness and badness are, indeed, matters of degree. But it does not follow that capacity for voluntary action is a matter of degree. If it were, we would have some kind of spectrum vocabulary for degrees of voluntariness similar to our vocabulary for degrees of rationality, (e.g., irrational, immature, foolish, reasonably sensible, fairly wise, very wise, etc.). But the fact is, we don't.

The reason why Strawson confuses the rationality condition with the voluntariness condition is probably that free agency is normally presupposed when the issue of rationality is raised. When free agency is presupposed, and only the degree, rather than the brute fact, of responsibility is in question (that is, were there extenuating circumstances?), the issue of determinism does appear irrelevant. But it ceases to be irrelevant as soon as the question of voluntary agency is reopened, for example, when, to use Strawson's own example, one person collides with another after being pushed by a third. The excuse of having been pushed, unlike that of immaturity or neurotic compulsion, negates the condition of free agency and thereby entirely eliminates responsibility, rather than indicating a low degree of rationality of the agent and thus merely reducing the degree of responsibility. It is no wonder then that determinism is irrelevant to degree of responsibility since, if determinism is true (and this is the cutting edge of hard determinism), the question of degree of responsibility simply cannot arise.

Strawson writes:

> It is not a consequence of any general thesis of determinism . . . that nobody knows what he's doing or that everybody's behavior is unintelligible in terms of conscious purpose or that nobody has a moral sense. . . . In fact no such sense of "determined" as would be required for a general thesis of determinism is ever relevant to our actual suspensions of moral reactive attitudes.[17]

Strawson is quite right to claim that *these* consequences do not follow from determinism, but he is wrong to conclude that *no* consequences follow for the fair assignment of moral responsibility. The consequences that do follow bear, not on the degree of rationality of the agent and thus on *degree* of responsibility, but on whether there is voluntary agency work at all, and thus on whether responsibility is relevant. If determinism is true, the answer to the latter question is no.

At the bottom of Strawson's argument for compatibilism lies a careless fallacy. The logical skeleton of his argument is this: Moral responsibility is a plain fact of life. Determinism may be true or it may be false—who knows? Therefore determinism cannot entail that no one is ever really responsible for what he or she does. This mode of reasoning resembles the following: The claim that the moon is made of Camembert cheese cannot entail that the moon is edible, because it is a plain fact that the moon is not edible. The conclusion we should draw from the obvious inedibility of the moon is not that the above entailment does not hold (it is a plain fact that it does) but that the minor premise of the inference, namely, that the moon is made of Camembert cheese, is false. Thus from his powerful case for the indispensability of the morally reactive attitudes, Strawson should have concluded that determinism is false, rather than that it does not entail non-responsibility.

Galen Strawson has tried to refute P. F. Strawson's argument for the indispensability of morally reactive attitudes like praise and blame, on the grounds that we can more easily do without them (as Buddhists claim to be able to do when they achieve enlightenment) than we can pay the more exorbitant cost of deep inconsistency between determinism about nature and libertarian indeterminism about human action.[18] But if we adopt the distinction I have proposed between dyadic, deterministic causality that applies in nature, and triadic, indeterministic causality that applies to voluntary action, the inconsistencies are avoided, and the cost is far lower than that of giving up all morally reactive attitudes, which amounts to moral suicide.

The M-N Dilemma and the Way Out

Of all the compatibilists I have read, I have found Dennett to be the most sensitive to the missing component needed to distinguish full-blooded voluntariness from pale tropistic simulation, and thus to see the need for adding a pinch of indeterminism to his mechanistic stew.[19] But I think he adds the wrong spice in the wrong place, in conflating the arbitrariness of the termination of deliberation[20] with the indeterminism of decision in the more centrally relevant sense of the ability to decide otherwise. According to Dennett, when reasons for various alternative courses of action have comparable weight, one may break a tie among them by means of a randomizing mechanism in the brain (like the toss of a die). But this cannot be the crucially indeterministic feature of decision-making, for it still does not account for the full-blooded desires that underlie voluntariness, and thus it still impales us on the deterministic horn of the M-N dilemma of predetermination versus randomness. (By the way, as Dennett himself recognizes, randomizing mechanisms do not, of themselves, rule out determinism.) On Dennett's account, the explanation of why one turns left rather than right at a fork in the road is that, so to speak, the die toss in one's head landed even rather than odd. That may be perfectly true for *intentionally arbitrary* selections such as an honorable duelist's selection of a weapon from a brace of pistols offered to him. But such arbitrary selections are hardly models of creative intelligence, nor do they illustrate the difference between full-blooded desires and tropisms, for the point of such arbitrary selections is precisely to deal with the fact that there is no greater desire for one alternative than for the other. The difference must be found in the agent's capacity to subdue or disregard the importunities of his or her dominant tendency if he or she has any (as contrasted with the heliotropic plant or the sphex wasp) and to do so for a reason that is brought into relevance by ones *revision* of one's priorities. It is, for example, the fact that Luther could conceivably have shrunk from the terrible consequences of breaking with the Church of Rome at the Diet of Worms, by deciding that the principles of *sole fide* was not, after all, as important as the unity of the church, that makes his act of defiance deserving of either blame or praise. Commenting on this case, Dennett draws the opposite conclusion,[21] namely, that we should take Luther's legendary declaration "I could no other" quite literally, thereby demonstrating that freely willed action does not entail that the agent could have done otherwise. (Frankfurt too misuses this example to make the same point.)[22] If Luther could have done otherwise, Dennett argues, "our sense of his moral strength would be severely diminished."[23] I think Dennett here conflates two specifications of "could have done oth-

32

erwise," namely, (*a*) Luther might have been cowardly enough to shrink from the fateful consequences of dividing the church out of fear for himself, and (*b*) he might have shrunk from them out of a not at all cowardly concern for the church and all its members, in judging that avoiding religious war is more important than preserving theological purity. The first sense of "could have . . ." manifests moral weakness, but the second sense does not. Insisting on (*a*) as the only relevant unpacking of "could have . . ." diverts attention from the fact that, without sense (*b*), involving the ability to revise one's priorities when confronted with grave problems stemming from one's present tendencies, creative intelligence would be frozen into tropistic routines from which random selection alone could not raise us to the level of responsible agency.

Crude compatibilists, from Hobbes to Ayer, argue for impaling ourselves on the determinist horn of the first-order M-N dilemma as a lesser evil than impaling ourselves on the randomness horn. To be free, they say, is not to be externally constrained, and in this sense to be able to do what one wants to do, whether or not one's desires are themselves predetermined. Sophisticated compatibilists like Armstrong, Henry, Frankfurt, and Dennett recognize that externally determined desires, that is, desires like hunger and thirst that are, on some occasions, such as intense biological need or hypnotic influence, not within the agent's voluntary control, are indistinguishable from tropisms and conditioned reflexes, and so they propose to go up one level, by defining freely willed action as involving second-order decision governed by the agent's long-range values as incorporated in his or her self-representation. But how much is really achieved by this ascent other than to postpone, rather than escape, the M-N dilemma? Are we not, on this second level, still confronted by the dilemma between predetermination and randomness? If so, then why is impalement here less painful than on the first level?

If not, then why has the dilemma melted away? Is it possible that decisions (which, I have argued, are not events separable from actions) are not qualified candidates on *either* level for either-predetermination or randomness? (John Hospers once made this suggestion with respect to the second level, but could not explain why it should be true on one level and false on another.[24] If so, then the dilemma is a false one on the first level, and we need not have made the ascent. We need not, and indeed cannot, coherently raise the question of whether a decision was causally predetermined. For there are no causal laws linking antecedent conditions to decisions that are features of actions rather than distinct events. Whatever laws, given initial conditions, entailed a decision to perform an action A would entail the occurrence of A itself, so that the alleged decision would not be a necessary condition for A, in which case A would not qualify as a voluntary action. The sophisticated compatibilist proposal that the decision to do A is not determined by initial conditions alone, but also involves a second-order decision that the first-order decision satisfies one's self-image or long-range values, only postpones the issue of whether decisions on *any* level are separable events capable of entering into causal laws.[25]

We can bring this abstract discussion down to earth by applying the first-order dilemma to concrete cases. There are people who rigidly stick to their rules of action regardless of consequences. We call then fanatics. There are others who disregard their professed rules whenever the consequences of following them would be painful or inconvenient. We call them moral weaklings. Just how tight is this disjunction? Is everyone either a fanatic or a moral weakling? Isn't there something in between, whichever level we are considering? (I suspect that the two levels, that of first-order decision to act and that of second-order decision as to whether a contemplated first-order decision is acceptable to one's ideal of self, or long-range values, have relevance to determining degree of rationality, but not to voluntariness.) Was Johann von Staupitz, Luther's vicar, morally weak in urging compromise, or was Luther fanatical in spurning compromise? We need not settle this religious controversy in order to see that the question is at least a sensible one, so that there must be some middle ground between inflexible determinism and capricious randomness symptomatic of moral weakness. Von Staupitz may possibly have been morally right rather than weak, and, on the other hand, Luther may possibly have been morally right rather than fanatical. Indeed, both may have been right.

Ed Sankowski, Gary Watson, Henry Frankfurt, and Daniel Dennett, among others, seem to subscribe to a concept of moral necessity that is not only compatible with determinism, but entails it.[26] And they would seem to have phenomenology on their side (countervailing C. A. Campbell's appeal to phenomenology as evidence for libertarian free will). We feel most free, they say, when we cannot imagine ourselves deciding any other way than the way we do decide. This is true, in a sense of "free," but is it the sense appropriate to moral responsibility? It might appear so since, as Sankowski, Dennett, and Watson point out, it is on just such occasions that we can be sure that a person's actions and decisions manifest her true character, that she is the kind of person who naturally acts and decides that way.

But does "naturally" here entail necessarily? I think not. Dennett claims that he, like all reasonably decent people, could not possibly commit a murder for profit. But I would give him more moral credit than he modestly gives himself. If the profit (say, as Dennett suggests, one thousand dollars) were the only means available for achieving an extraordinarily worthwhile end such as supplying food to a famine-devastated area, would he not be tempted to take out a smugly comfortable bureaucrat who stood in the way? Suppose he

35

and the official were driving through Ethiopia in a truck loaded with food and water for an extended safari, and they saw hundreds of starving children begging for nourishment. And suppose the truck belonged to the official, who coldly refused Dennett's pleas that the food and water be distributed to the starving children. If the only way Dennett could save the children was to shoot the official, would he not be tempted to do so, and would it not be evidence of moral insensibility not to be so tempted?

The reason Dennett's compatibilist phenomenological argument appears plausible is that there is a sense of "free" that applies here, but it is not the sense that grounds responsibility. I have in mind freedom from conflict and indecision. When we are most free in this sense, we feel an intoxicating surge of power and purposefulness, and this is one of our most cherished experiences. But it has nothing to do with the objective ground of moral responsibility, since it is just as vividly present in morally neutral contexts, such as free-fall parachuting, pursing one's chosen career, or acquiring complex skills such as musical virtuosity.

When one is able to decide without hesitation born of countervailing reasons, does this show that one could not have decided otherwise and thus constitute a refutation of the categorical interpretation of "could have done otherwise," as the above compatibilists hold? I think not. This point may be argued in two ways:

1. On the hypothetical interpretation of "could have decided otherwise," favored by compatibilists, it is easy to see that freedom from psychic conflict and indecision does not entail necessitation of action. Obviously, if one had a good reason to decide otherwise, one would have done so, and therefore could have done so. It is interesting to note how compatibilists tend to abandon their hypothetical

interpretation of "could" in favor of the libertarian categorical interpretation in this context, where their axe seems more sharply ground on the latter.

2. On the categorical interpretation of "could have decided otherwise," it is less obvious that, when we are free from indecision due to conflicting reasons, we are also free to decide otherwise. And that is why we are likely to say, with Luther, "I could no other." We cannot imagine ourselves making the crazy decision to do what we can see no reason for doing, except by supposing ourselves to be someone else, which would be irrelevant in this context, or else as having different reasons for action, which would contradict the initial hypothesis.

This point must, I think, be conceded by libertarians of any shape or form. One cannot imagine oneself rationally, in one's right mind, so to speak, deciding to do what one sees no reason to do and very good reason not to do. But surely one can imagine oneself lapsing into irrationality, being suddenly seized by an imp of the perverse, or perhaps, like St. Paul on the road to Damascus, having a vision that changes one's perspective and reveals reasons for action that were previously not there. Would this latter case contradict the hypothesis that one has no reason for deciding otherwise? Only if what was meant was that one could not possibly have a reason, but surely that claim is so strong as to be utterly implausible in the cases cited by Dennett et al. Recall the argument earlier that the full-blooded concept of desire implies the possibility, at least, of countervailing desires, and that of rationality implies the possibility of reorganizing one's priorities in response to previously unforseen contingencies.

I must confess some misgivings about the conclusiveness of the above reasoning, because I am somewhat doubtful about the meaningfulness of "could have decided otherwise" as contrasted with "could have *done* otherwise." "X decided to do A," I have argued, entails that X could (categorically) have done other than A or at least refrained from doing A. And if X had refrained of his own free will from doing A, then X must have decided to refrain. It follows that X could have so decided. For one always can do what in fact one intentionally does. But all this talk seems to presuppose that the decision to do A is some kind of mental act distinct from the doing of A, which is what I argued against in the earlier discussion of trigger causes. I maintained that deciding to do A is just doing A voluntarily, or at least trying to do A, when it is not merely provisional and revocable, and thus a merely dispositional condition that cannot be a trigger cause. So if one is neither a fanatic nor a moral weakling, one could do otherwise and, if one could (intentionally) do otherwise, then of course one could decide otherwise, even when an alternative decision is so unlikely as to be difficult to imagine. So we hardly need argument 2 above, with its apparently unacceptable presupposition that decisions are distinct mental events. To deflect the cutting edge of the compatibilist argument from resoluteness we need only grant that (*a*) it is extremely unlikely that the resolute agent would decide otherwise, and (*b*) if, however, so unlikely an event were to occur after all, that would manifest either a sudden lapse from rationality, or a radical conversion, or some such abnormal phenomenon, and then, after making these concessions, we can still hold that, exceptional as these qualifications may be, they conform to the categorical interpretation of "could have done (or decided) otherwise."

We may, I think, conclude that the Melden-Nagel dilemma is illusory on both levels—that of action and that of second-order evaluation of first-order decisions to act. Decisions are neither predetermined in a law-like manner nor, except in special cases calling for arbitrary selection (like the honorable duelist), randomly generated.

When, because of the fanatical inflexibility of the agent, they approach the extreme of rule fetishism, we are tempted to see them (metaphorically, I suggest) as cases of causal predetermination, and when, because of the moral weakness of the agent, they approach the extreme of wantonness (to use Frankfurt's felicitous term), we are tempted to see them as cases of randomly generated impulse. But both temptations should be resisted for taking metaphors too literally. For even fanatics and wantons are not automata. Even they could, conceivably, do otherwise, and are therefore subject to moral appraisal.

We should conclude that the M-N dilemma does not apply to voluntary action on any level. Decisions and the actions they characterize are neither predetermined in a regular pattern, nor randomly generated. When they are too rigidly rule-governed we consider the agent a fanatic; when not rule-governed at all we suspect moral weakness or caprice. But even fanatics, weaklings, and wantons are not incapable of deciding otherwise. Recall that the presupposition from which the M-N dilemma followed was that, given the antecedent conditions of action, only one outcome is possible. That presupposition in turn rests on the assumption that, if action is caused, the causality involved is dyadic. If we recognize that psychological causality is triadic and therefore indeterministic, we need no longer presuppose only one possible outcome, and then the dilemma disappears. This seems to me a very good reason to accept the proposed distinction between the two types of causality. We shall see in subsequent chapters that other benefits follow as well.

Postscript

I think I owe the reader an explanation of the difference between the hypothetical interpretation of "could have done otherwise" and the categorical interpretation that I have defended in this chapter. The hypothetical interpretation was first explicitly stated by G. E. Moore, but all compatibilists have implicitly employed it and all incompatibilists have rejected it, so that it lies at the heart of the free will controversy. It is, simply, that "X could have done otherwise" means that X *would* have done otherwise if certain conditions had obtained, such as: if the agent had had a better character, or had given more thought to the consequences, and so on, where the counterfactual condition implied is the sort of thing that can be affected by the threat of blame or punishment.

The categorical interpretation is the insistence that no such conditional unpacking does justice to the mean of "could" relevant to moral responsibility; "could have done otherwise" means just what it says and nothing else.

3

WHERE THE BUCK STOPS AND WHY

The T-R Principle

At the beginning of Charlie Chaplin's cinematic masterpiece *The Great Dictator,* an allied World War I shell falls behind the German lines and fails to explode. The commanding officer orders his second-in-command to dispose of the shell before it goes off. The second-in-command hands the shell to his subaltern, who in turn hands it to the next-in-line, until it reaches Charlie, who turns to hand it on when he suddenly realizes there is no one lower than himself. The buck stopped with Charlie.

This is a distinctively Prussian way of transferring responsibility—namely, by pulling rank. There are myriad other ways, some more appropriate than others to specific kinds of responsibility. I would like here to consider causal transfer from effect to cause, because we can, I think, make sense of this familiar phenomenon only if we employ the suggested distinction between triadic and dyadic causality.

Following up the distinction made in Chapter 1 between two kinds of causality, I propose that we distinguish two kinds of causal chains, which I shall call "natural" chains and "action" chains. By a natural causal chain, I mean a sequence of events, each of which is the effect of its predecessor (if it has one) and the cause of its successor (if it has one), and none of which is an intentional human action. By an action chain I mean a sequence of events at least one of which is an intentional human action and is similarly causally ordered. Parts of either kind of chain will be called segments. A segment of an action chain will be either an action segment or a natural segment, depending on whether it does or does not include at least one intentionable action.

I think the above distinction between natural and action chains or segments is acceptable to all sides of the free will controversy. Hard determinists may consider it superficial, since they think that the difference cuts no metaphysical or ethical ice, but there is no reason for them to deny that intentional actions are in some ways different from other kinds of events. They merely insist that no assignments of responsibility can be justified by whatever those differences may be. Soft determinists, and compatibilists who are agnostic about determinism, insist on the importance of the distinction as the ground for ascribing and denying moral responsibility, but they claim that the difference is not to be found in the degree of tightness of the causal bond involved. Thus they deny precisely what I shall try to establish in this chapter, namely, that while natural causal segments are (with the possible exception of subatomic events) deterministic—each link necessitating its successor—an action segment is indeterministic insofar as the cause of an intentional action need not be followed by its effect, because whether the action is performed depends not only on its cause but also on the choice or decision of the agent. How exactly the difference between natural and action chains is to be explained by compatibilists is their problem. I will try to show that they cannot explain the difference in a way consistent with our assignments and transferences of moral responsibility.

In some earlier papers, I formulated a rule that I believe we usually follow in assigning and disclaiming responsibility—a rule that I call the Principle of Transferability of Responsibility, or, in brief, T-R, as follows: Whoever is not responsible for bringing about the cause of an event is not responsible for bringing about its effect and, contrapositively, whoever *is* responsible for bringing about the effect of a cause must have been responsible for bringing about its cause. It is in accordance with this principle that one passes the buck of moral responsibility when one protests: "It wasn't my fault; someone else did it." T-R resembles the *beta* rule formulated by Peter van Inwagen in his book *An Essay on Free Will*,[1] and, like his rule, it seems to support the inference, which van Inwagen draws explicitly, that responsibility for events along infinite causal chains is ancestrally transferable *ad infinitum*, so that if, as determinists hold, all events lie on such chains, then no one is ever responsible for anything. Kurt Baier calls this inference the Argument from Ultimate Nonresponsibility, and he claims that it commits a fallacy by equivocating on different senses of responsibility.[2] I shall say more about Baier's argument a little later. First I would like to examine my T-R principle more closely in the light of the distinction I have drawn between natural causal chains and action chains.

When we consider a natural causal chain, T-R seems clearly to hold. Consider, for instance, the following example: A brick falls from a roof, striking a car, which goes out of control, snapping a telephone pole, which falls against a house and then demolishes its roof. Who is morally responsible for demolishing the roof? Not the driver of the car, surely, but whoever dislodged the brick, if anyone did; otherwise, no one is responsible. (Needless to say, I am not here concerned with legal liability.)

However, if we consider an action chain, T-R appears clearly false. For example, if a government official is bribed by an airplane manufacturer to accept defective fighter planes, some of which crash because of their defects, the official may not argue that the resultant casualties were not his fault but the fault of the manufacturer, on the ground that his own corrupt conduct was caused or brought about by the manufacturer's offer of a bribe. Some slight degree of responsibility may here be transferred from effect to cause, but precious little; this is more a matter of sharing responsibility than of transferring it. Both the official and the manufacturer belong in jail.

T-R thus appears true for natural chains or segments but false for action chains or segments. Indeed, it seems trivially true for natural chains since what it asserts is that whoever did not bring about the cause of an event was not responsible for bringing about the event in question, insofar as bringing about the event was accomplished by bringing about its cause. That one can't be responsible for doing what one didn't do seems patently tautologous.

We need not worry here about the alleged difference between so-called basic actions that are simply performed without doing something else to bring them about and complex actions in which some things are done to bring about other things. Whether or not there are absolutely basic actions (I am inclined to think there are, but I am not prepared to argue the matter here), we can use the phrase "bring about" to include the special case of just doing, if there is such a special case. It doesn't in any way affect the main line of reasoning.

Types of Responsibility

Let us now take a closer look at the concept of responsibility and its behavior along both types of causal chains. There are several different although closely related senses of "responsibility" that are all too easy to confuse. The differences between legal and moral responsibility are the most obvious, but even these are sometimes overlooked.

Legal responsibility is imposed according to explicit and socially agreed upon rules, and it is transferable from one agent to another according to those rules. Moral responsibility is less dependent on such explicit conventions, nor can it be so easily transferred, but here again one must make distinctions. Responsibilities that are entailed by universal moral duties of the strict sort emphasized by Kant are not voluntarily assumed, renounced, or transferred to others. Responsibility for violating a strict duty not to take life, steal, or otherwise abuse the rights of others develops within the psyche of each human child almost as naturally as his wisdom teeth grow with age and exercise. There is still a difference here between the social and the biological, in that there remains a subtle but crucial element of convention in the former; for human beings who renounce membership in all kinds of communities and prefers to live as hermits in the wilderness may refuse to acknowledge convention or, having previously acknowledged it, may then renounce their moral responsibilities toward others, like Moliere's Misanthrope at the end of the play.

Within the very broad category of moral responsibility we can distinguish at least two subclasses with respect to two important properties: degree of obligatoriness or ethical precedence, and degree of ease of assumption, renunciation, and transference. These two subclasses are universal moral responsibilities and special responsibilities connected with one's personal relationships and one's social roles. Universal responsibilities that every adult person bears toward every contemporary and, to a lesser extent, even toward posterity can themselves be divided, as Kant did, between strict and meritorious duties or those of perfect and those of imperfect obligations, which Philippa Foot has aptly renamed duties of justice and duties of charity. The transferability conditions of these subclasses of responsibility vary considerably.

45

The general concept of moral responsibility is itself somewhat ambiguous, as Kurt Baier, Jonathan Glover, Herbert Fingarette, and other have pointed out.[3] Baier distinguishes three senses: accountability, answerability, and culpability. Accountability corresponds to the kind of moral responsibility we attribute to people as a virtue, as when we say of someone that she is a responsible person, or of a small child that she has not yet reached the age to *take* responsibility in Baier's second sense, namely, answerability. The latter, Baier suggests, devolves upon a person in accordance with the "rules of the practice of bringing people to account," and consists in being required to justify, excuse, or accept blame for violations of such rules. Culpability is that form of responsibility that consists in being subject to justifiable blame and/or punishment. Obviously, accountability is a necessary but not sufficient condition for culpability. The additional condition for answerability is that the subject appear to have violated a moral rule; and the additional condition for culpability is that the subject lack justification and excuse.

Baier thinks that attention to these different senses of responsibility supports the compatibility of causal determinism with moral responsibility. He argues that transferability along a causal chain applies only to culpability, not to accountability, while determinism entails only that accountability, not culpability, can be traced back beyond the circumstances over which the agent has control. A person must be accountable in order to be culpable, and one's culpability entails that one's actions are neither justifiable nor excusable, but it does not entail that, given one's character and circumstances, one could have refrained from his wrongful action. Thus culpability, according to Baier, is *not* ancestrally transferable along a causal chain; it seems so only when we confuse culpability with accountability.

Baier is here arguing against John Hospers, who held that one has no control over the formation of one's own character and consequently one is not culpable for having developed a bad character and therefore not culpable for the bad actions that are causally necessitated by one's bad character. Baier is quite right to point out, in rebuttal of Hospers, that culpability for one's actions does not entail culpability for one's character. But this rebuttal is relevant only to those who, like Hospers and Baier, assume that the sense of "cause" in which a character trait can be said to cause (or at least be a causal factor of) a person's action is the same as that in which a surge of voltage can be said to cause a fuse to melt—in brief, that psychological causality is deterministic. But if that were true, then although, as Baier rightly argues, culpability need not be indefinitely transferable, it would also be the case, unnoted by Baier, that culpability would never be justly ascribable at all, and hard determinism would be vindicated.

Is it true, as Baier claims, that culpability is not indefinitely transferable backward along a causal chain? Consider a chain of events beginning with a voluntary action and culminating in harm to an innocent victim: X does A, which causes B, which causes C, which causes injury to Y. For example, a vandal throws a glass bottle from an overpass onto a highway; the bottle strikes the windshield of a passing car, sending it out of control into the path of an oncoming car, resulting in a collision that seriously injures both drivers. The blame, and probably also the punishment, does not rest with the two drivers, nor with the deadly bottle, but passes to the vandal who initiated the chain of events. Had the bottle fallen from a hillside when dislodged by a gust of wind, there would be no one to blame except perhaps, as Hume suggested, the ultimate Author of all causal chains, which is probably why such accidental harms are called "acts of God" in the quaint jargon of the lawcourts.

It is obvious enough why responsibility as culpability for harm gets transferred back to the initiator of a causal chain. We do not hold insentient beings like bottles morally responsible for the harm they cause, because they do not *initiate* the causal chains in which they play a role, nor do we assign responsibility in the sense of culpability to humans when their responses are non-voluntary reflexes over which they have no rational control. In such cases we regard the human agents as not significantly different from insentient objects. So we trace backward along the causal chain until we reach a voluntary action and that is where the buck stops. If, no matter how far back we trace the causal chain, we find no voluntary action initiating the chain, then culpability does not apply anywhere along the chain. Now what do such chains have in common in virtue of which there is no one to blame? Their common feature is that they are chains of *natural* causation, along which no voluntary actions of rational agents are to be found. They are also deterministic, or law-governed sequences of events. Is there a connection between these two features? I suggest that there is, in fact—that these two features are coextensive. A deterministic causal chain (setting aside subatomic events, whose very status as events is doubtful) is a chain of natural causes and effects, while a chain initiated by a voluntary action is an indeterministic chain. Where mind is at work, lawlessness is rampant.

Transferring Culpability

Like all compatibilists, Baier holds that culpability has nothing to do with the remote events that formed an agent's character, but only with whether or not the agent, in performing a harmful action, had an excuse such as ignorance, coercion, or inner compulsion. It would be helpful to distinguish, as Baier does not, between two importantly different kinds of excusing conditions: those such as coercion and psychic compulsion, which only partly mitigate culpability, and those that completely exculpate precisely because they indicate that no voluntary action was involved, or that the voluntary action that the agent, through no fault of her own, believed she was performing was not what actually occurred. An example of the first would be the case of the driver who swerves when her windshield is struck by a bottle. An example of the second is any non-negligent case of unintentionally causing harm, as when one has no way of knowing that the Tylenol capsules contain cyanide. In both cases, the causal chain is not initiated by a voluntary action, whereas, in cases where excusing conditions only partly mitigate culpability, the initiating action is voluntary but insufficiently rational to justify ascribing full culpability.

Completely excusing conditions such as uncontrollable reflex and non-negligent ignorance require us to transfer culpability backward along a deterministic causal chain to the initiator, if there was one. Partially excusing conditions like coercion, psychic compulsion, and immaturity involve more complex conditions of transfer of culpability. Depending on the kind of excuse involved and on other circumstances, culpability may be: (*a*) largely but not entirely transferable backward along the causal chain, as when an adult exerts an evil influence over a child, like Fagan over Oliver Twist, or when a soldier is coerced by threat of torture into revealing military secrets (the soldier may be partially to blame for not holding out longer, but the major part of the blame belongs to the torturer); (*b*) equally and fully shared, as when two men engage in a gun duel and a bystander is injured; (*c*) partially but, I think, only slightly transferable, where the agent is interpreting the instructions of a higher authority, as is usually the case in the occurrence of wartime atrocities.

During the undeclared war in Vietnam, President Lyndon Johnson instructed General William Westmoreland to intensify efforts to "pacify" the rural areas of South Vietnam. Westmoreland ordered his subordinate officers to conduct "search and destroy" missions among suspect villages, and they in turn demanded high "body counts" from their subordinates. Lieutenant William Calley interpreted these instructions to signify that he should require his platoon to shoot down unarmed women and children. Who was to blame, and how should the blame have been distributed? Lieutenant Calley argued in his defense at the subsequent court-martial that all the blame should be transferred to his immediate superior, Captain Medina. Some political writers particularly on the left, held that most of the blame should be transferred backward along the chain of authority either to General Westmoreland or even beyond him to President Johnson. The officers who sat in judgment at the court-martial concluded that, according to the military manual, Lieutenant Calley could not properly interpret the "high body count" instructions as justifying the murder of unarmed civilians and that, in any case, he had a moral and military duty to refuse to obey any such order, as did the Nazi officers condemned at Nuremberg. Many critics protested this judgment, arguing that assigning all the culpability to Lieutenant Calley was an injustice designed to protect the policy makers who created a climate in which such atrocities were likely to occur. Which side is right? I believe that both sides were partly right. The military court was right to hold that Lieutenant Calley bore the primary responsibility for what he did, that is, for ordering the execution of unarmed prisoners. But the policy set by President Johnson, the Joint Chiefs of Staff, and General Westmoreland could have been expected to encourage such atrocities, by influencing men in the field to regard apparent noncombatants with hostility and fear. In rewarding high body counts, the policy tempted soldiers to shoot first and ask questions later. Nevertheless, the policy did not *necessitate* atrocities, as evidenced by the fact that few such cases came to light.

On the other hand, the critics of the Calley verdict were right to hold that the policy makers were even more culpable than Lieutenant Calley. They were not more culpable for the particular atrocity of My lai, which he, not they, perpetrated. They were only slightly culpable for having influenced (but not, as the court rightly judged, necessitated) that and other abominations. But if we add up (in whatever non-mathematical method of summation applies to ethics) the slight culpability of the framers of military policy for each of the deaths, mutilations, and deprivations inflicted on the noncombatants of that war-ravaged country, their total culpability exceeds by far that of Lieutenant Calley. Needless to say, this consideration reduces Calley's culpability by so slight an amount that it should have afforded little comfort to his apologists, anymore than growing up in a crime-ridden ghetto significantly reduces a juvenile delinquent's culpability for vicious crimes.

It would be hard to achieve general agreement on assignments of culpability in cases so politically controversial, but whichever side one is inclined to support, it seems clear that, while some portion of responsibility is transferable from the proximate agent backward along the causal chain of command, not all of it is—in my opinion very little, in the opinion of some quite a bit, but in almost no one's opinion all.

The difference we have found among conditions and degrees of transference of culpability seem to me to show that culpability is completely transferable from effect to cause along a *deterministic* segment in which no intermediate links are voluntary actions, but not so along an action segment in which the links are voluntary actions of human agents. If we bear in mind the point made earlier,

51

that fully excusing conditions such as uncontrollable reflex, derangement, and non-negligent ignorance remove the controversial event from the category of voluntary action, then it follows that although Baier is right to hold that culpability is not indefinitely transferable backward along an *action segment,* he is wrong to hold that it is not ancestrally transferable along a natural causal segment. But if voluntary action were, as determinists claim, as rigorously determined by character as is the melting of a fuse by excessive voltage, then culpability *would* be transferable à la d'Holbach and Hospers, from action to character and from character to its causes, and the buck would never stop except perhaps with the Creator. If on the other hand, voluntary action breaks the transferability of culpability, then it does so by breaking the deterministic causal chain and cannot be claimed to be necessitated by character. Baier simply cannot have it *both* ways, nor can others like Edward Sankowski, who, in a 1980 essay, after cogently distinguishing the alleged causal relation between character and action from that between natural cause and effect, draws the implausible *non sequitur* that both relations are equally "necessary" in some undefined sense of "necessary," and concludes that moral responsibility is compatible with determinism.[4] I have yet to find a form of compatibilism that does not commit some such fallacy by regarding action chains as similar to natural causal chains for the purposes of determinism, while also insisting that they are importantly different for the purposes of ascribing responsibility.

Let us take stock. Have I proven conclusively that action chains are not deterministic causal chains? No, I have not, nor do I think it possible to do so. I have only tried to show that it is implausible to regard action chains as deterministic causal chains. My reasoning, in a nutshell, is this: *If* action chains were as deterministic as natural chains, then there wouldn't be any *point* to having different and more complex conditions of transferability of responsibility along the two types of chains, differences appealed to by compatibilists like Baier and Strawson when they want to escape the embarrassing consequences drawn by hard determinists like d'Holbach and Hospers.

Alternative Accounts of Transfers of Culpability

Some determinists, among them P. H. Nowell-Smith, R. B. Hobart, J. C. Smart, Dennett, and Glover, have maintained that there is, after all, a point to having different T-R conditions for the two types of causal chains, even if both types are deterministic.[5] The point, they say, of holding people responsible for what they do, but not for what happens to them, is to deter them from doing what we don't want them to do, such as lying, stealing, assaulting, breaking promises, and so on. This, they argue, far from implying that the actions of responsible agents are not determined by antecedent causes, implies the contrary—that the threat of blame and punishment will add to the causal force of their own stirrings of conscience and so reinforce their inhibitions against socially disapproved actions as to cause them to refrain from such actions. Holding people culpable, in this sense of threatening them with blame and punishment, thus provides them with a compelling reason to desist, a reason that consists in the belief that one may be blamed or punished, together with the desire to avoid those unpleasant consequences. A reason so compelling may then be considered the effective cause that deters wrong action.

There are two mistakes in the above account:

1. Whether or not a person is morally responsible or culpable for a harmful action is not at all the same as whether that person is *held* responsible by others. Morally innocent people are all too

often blamed and punished. Nor does the threat of sanctions make people morally culpable. What makes people morally culpable is the moral fact that their harmful action is voluntary, rational, and inexcusable, rather than the social fact that others threaten them with sanctions. The latter fact is relevant only to legal, not to moral responsibility.

2. On the view that all causality is deterministic, if deterrence were the point of blame and punishment, then the wrong people would be blamed and punished—namely, those who, in committing the wrongful actions, were *not* deterred from their mischievous course. To this objection the compatibilist will no doubt reply that the goal of deterrence is achieved by the *threat* of sanctions, and that the purpose of carrying out the sanctions is merely to uphold the credibility of the threat. But if so, then it follows that those who are blamed and punished are not really those against whom the threat of sanctions is directed. The former are incorrigibles for whom we ought to have sympathetic understanding, rather than make them sacrificial lambs to uphold the credibility of our laws. Convicted criminals on this view are martyrs who do not deserve the suffering we inflict on them for the utilitarian purpose of deterring more rational potential wrongdoers who, because of their superior rationality, always manage to escape blame and punishment. In brief, if the point of ascribing moral responsibility is to cause people to refrain from wrongful action *in a deterministic sense of "cause,"* then our procedure is woefully unjust, because only those who are *not* deserving of the sanctions receive them.

An escape from this paradox is to return to the common sense belief that, aside from occasional errors of judgment, those who are blamed and punished deserve their fate because they could have refrained from wrongdoing, threats or no threats, and those who refrain deserve the respect due all law-abiding people because they could have done wrong. In brief, whatever causal influence the threat of sanctions has on rational agents should be considered as a link on an action chain, not as a link on a deterministic causal chain, if we are to make coherent sense of our morally reactive attitudes.

4

EXTRA CREDIT AND DISCREDIT

The Parable of the Prodigal Son

Compatibilism on the issue of free will versus determinism, I have argued, has difficulty accounting for common sense ascriptions, transferences, and divisions of responsibility. I now want to make the further point that it cannot account for still another phenomenon of our everyday moral experience: the surges of special admiration or contempt that we often feel toward those who exceed or fall short of the moral expectations to which their past patterns of conduct have given rise. The words "credit" and "discredit" may grate on the nerves of readers who dislike commercial metaphors in moral discourse, suggestive as they are of the religious glorification of mercenary virtues like thrift and productive efficiency that Max Weber found to be the spirit of early capitalism. But in the context of this discussion, we can always replace them with less commercial-sounding terms like degrees of approval or disapproval. Personally, I prefer the terms "credit" and "discredit" because they are more suggestive of objective desert, but nothing turns, I think, on which words we use. I am trying to find the rational ground for extra approval of unexpected reforms and extra disapproval of unexpected lapses, above and beyond the degree of approval or disapproval considered to be merited by the good deeds of the generally virtuous and the misdeeds of the generally miscreant.

The Parable of the Prodigal Son in the gospel according to Luke is commonly believed to convey an ethical lesson.[1] It certainly strikes a responsive chord in one's moral feelings. But just what its lesson is does not seem to me at all clear. There are a number of puzzling features that obscure rather than illuminate the moral of the story. Here are the salient details:

A well-to-do farmer has two sons. One day the younger son asks for his inheritance, receives it, and takes off for a distant city, where he squanders his fortune in dissolute living. Reduced to penury, sickness, and hunger, he makes his way home, where his father welcomes him joyously, dresses him in costly raiment, and orders a fatted calf killed for an evening feast. The prodigal son, who has rehearsed this scene in advance, throws himself at his father's feet and declares himself unworthy to be his son. When the elder brother comes home from the fields, he refuses to join in the celebration, complaining to his father that a fatted calf had never been killed for him, to which the father replies that the younger brother had been lost and now was found, so naturally they should celebrate.

Commentators on this parable usually interpret it as symbolizing the celebration of the reform of a sinner, the kind father representing God and the farm the Kingdom of the Blessed.[2] The elder son is considered mean-spirited and self-righteous, like the Pharisees who scolded Jesus for consorting with publicans, prostitutes, and other riffraff.

One question that puzzles me is why the prodigal son is described as driven home by famine and as rehearsing his self-denunciation in advance. These two details suggest that his change of heart was calculated and his expressions of humility insincere. Are we to admire the father for not noticing the dissimulation or are we to conclude that he and God are glad to get sinners back by hook or crook, no questions asked? That might be an understandable weakness in a human father but the Divine Father is not supposed to have weaknesses.

Could the ethical-religious lesson of the parable really be that any return to the fold, with the mere appearance of penitence, no matter how calculated, will be received with joy and celebration? Such an interpretation seems unacceptably crude. Yet it is further supported by the context of the parable, which appears in Luke as the third of a series of three recited by Jesus in answer to the criticism of the Pharisees. Jesus first describes a sheepherder who searches for a stray sheep and on finding it, cradles it in his arms, caring more for this one maverick than for the ninety-nine who never strayed. Next he tells of a woman who had ten gold coins, loses one, and upon finding it again invites her neighbors to a party to celebrate her good fortune. Then comes the parable of the Prodigal Son. Some writers have speculated that perhaps the original order of the parables was accidentally changed, since the sequence inanimate (coin)–animal (sheep)–human (son) is the more appropriate sequence, while others insist that the present sequence is correct in view of the mathematical progression one hundred sheep, ten coins, two sons, which represent the increasing value of each item.[3] The trouble with either order is that it treats as similar, if unequal in value, sheep, coins, and sons as if all were treasured possessions so that the return of each is to be celebrated as a stroke of good luck; but the starvation, illness, and humiliation that overcame the prodigal son can hardly be so regarded by a kind and loving father.

Another matter that puzzles me is why the elder son's protest is put as a jealous complaint rather than as doubt about the sincerity of the prodigal's reform. The latter objection would have merited more careful consideration by the father. Not that the father would have had no reasonable response available. He could have replied that even conceding a selfish motive for the prodigal's return and the possible insincerity of his self- denunciation, still one may have faith in the possibility that he has learned his lesson and will, in his future conduct, reaffirm and fulfill his initially calculated promise of reform. It is not easy to change one's character; it takes time and constant practice to rebuild what one has allowed to fall into extreme disrepair. The initiation of the process of rebuilding calls for considerable effort that merits appreciation and encouragement, whatever the circumstances that occasioned it.

Setting aside these puzzling details, the image of the sinner receiving special credit for an effort to reform is, I think, what touches us most and makes the story so appealing that it has been called the "pearl and crown of the parables."[4] It is, I think, an important fact of moral experience that we feel prompted to give sinners extra credit for their attempts at reform and, on the other side of the coin, that we tend to give generally well-behaved people extra discredit when they let us down. This is the puzzle that I would like to explore: why *extra* credit for the reformed sinner and *extra* discredit for the fallen saint, above and beyond the normal credit or discredit that, in the first case, a good action and, in the second case, a bad action, considered in themselves, would merit? This would be a sympathetic interpretation of the elder brother's complaint in the parable, one that would call for a straight answer rather than an *ad hominem* put-down. When I was growing up I was a fairly docile child, unlike my wayward older brother, and I recall that on the few occasions we got out of line together, I was more severely scolded than my brother for the same offense. Like the elder brother in the parable, I felt that this unequal treatment was unjust. But I no longer feel that way; on the contrary, I find myself responding in the same unequal way to my own children and I therefore think it worth looking for a rational ground for this phenomenon of extra credit and discredit.

It might be thought that in looking for a rational ground, I am asking for too much because the tendency to delight in being favorable surprised by a sinner's reform and the tendency to be especially indignant at unexpected misdeeds of people we trust are simply facts of human nature having nothing to do with moral credit or discredit. The father of the prodigal son was happy to have him back: why look any deeper into the matter? But if our responses to such events have nothing to do with moral merit or demerit, then such unequal responses, natural though they may be, are unfair and the elder son in the parable had a case worth pleading and so did I with respect to the apparent favoritism shown to my own brother. Yet my feeling now is that my parents were in the right and so is the father in the parable and I want to justify this feeling by articulating its rational ground.

To highlight the issue, free of distracting details, I shall take the liberty of simplifying the parable by assuming the prodigal son to have returned home voluntarily, genuinely prompted by remorse. Would he then deserve the fatted calf that his elder brother had not merited despite all his years of faithful service? The common conviction that he would might be explained in three different ways as follows.

Reinforcement, Compensation, and Moral Effort

1. It might be said that a reformed sinner requires special encouragement to persevere in resisting the temptations to which he has been habituated. The motivation to change for the better, initially sparked by boredom with one's sinful life and by the excitement of sudden change, tends to flag with time and needs to be reinforced by

special rewards for good conduct. We might call this explanation the "reinforcement theory." The defect of this account is that it fails to answer the elder son's complaint that special rewards for reformed sinners are unfair to those of constant virtue. Indeed, they give the virtuous reason to sin occasionally in order to reap similar extra dividends. Moreover, reinforcement, if not deserved, looks suspiciously like bribery.

2. Extra credit for the reformed sinner and extra discredit for the fallen saint might be explained as compensation for having underrated or overrated their character in the past. It might be held that just because the sinner's reform was unexpected, we feel that there must have been more good in him or her than we had realized, so that we owe them extra credit as compensation for the excessive discredit they had suffered in our eyes. Conversely, when persons of well-regarded character commit crimes we realize that we have given them too much credit in the past and so we blame or punish them not only for their misdeeds but additionally to compensate ourselves at their expense for past overpayments of moral credit.

This compensation theory sounds deplorably like the bookkeeping morality for which Nietzsche and Spengler criticized protestant ethics. But it comes closer than the reinforcement theory to a moral explanation of the phenomenon of extra credit and discredit, although it does not quite reach its goal. It has the merit of satisfying one criterion of fairness in that it provides a ground for considering the extra credit or discredit as owed to the recipient. But it violates a second and equally weighty criterion of fairness in assigning credit or discredit to a feature of the agent that is antecedent to her action in addition to the action for which she is being praised or blamed. Suppose a thief has an opportunity to steal with impunity but, on an impulse to reform, resists the temptation. Is he to be praised for what he had been—that is, for being a thief with a capacity to reform, as well as for what his forbearance shows him to be now, a reformed thief? Suppose a heretofore honest banker falls in love with his secretary and embezzles funds to take her to Acapulco. Is he to be blamed for not having been honest enough to be incapable of falling into temptation in addition to being blamed for not resisting the temptation? Are we to deduct past credit from the banker and award it to the thief, thereby erasing the moral difference between their past lives? That strikes me as a gratuitous rewriting of the past in the light of the present—a kind of double jeopardy for the banker and a double redemption for the thief.

3. The idea of moral effort provides a third explanation of extra credit and discredit, one that seems to me far more plausible than the first two. It is easy for a person of good character to behave well; consequently, that person merits less praise or reward for good deeds and more discredit for evil deeds. Conversely, it is more difficult for one of weak character to resist temptation and such resistance deserves extra credit. C. A. Campbell has made this point eloquently in an essay that has not received the attention it deserves.[5] Moral effort, he observes, varies inversely with natural inclination. It takes less moral effort to be good if one is so inclined since the more strongly one is tempted, the more effort is required to resist. What is interesting about this fact, Campbell points out, is that it seems to contradict deterministic views of human action such as that of John Stuart Mill, according to which people necessarily act to satisfy their strongest desire.[6] If that were true, moral effort would have no role to play in the explanation of human conduct.

More sophisticated forms of determinism seem to allow for the role of moral effort as a higher-order type of motivation that causally explains unexpectedly good conduct. For example, Harry Frankfurt explains successful resistance to one's strongest desire in terms of the inhibiting effect of a second-order desire stemming from a person's self-image and long-range purposes.[7] Freedom of the will, for him, consists in the ability to act on one's second-order desires to satisfy those first-order desires of which one approves and to inhibit those of which one disapproves. Frankfurt's distinction between first- and second-order desires explains plausibly why we do not hold animals, small children, or the mentally defective morally responsible for their actions in that they lack a clear enough self-image and plan of life to be able to form efficacious second-order desires. However, with respect to moral effort and extra credit, his causal account only postpones, but does not solve, our problem. For we must still explain why someone like the prodigal son or Frankfurt's "wanton," whose long-range purpose is to satisfy his first-order desires, can unexpectedly revise his long-range or second-order goal for the better, and deserves extra credit for doing so. Once again we seem to need the notion of moral effort somehow overcoming even the second-order desires of which the agent has come to disapprove. If we then appeal to a third-order level of desires, we teeter on the edge of an infinite regress.

It seems to me that any deterministic account of moral effort is bound to reduce it to something that plays the wrong kind of explanatory role. Even Campbell finally makes this mistake when he tries to explain effort of the will as a kind of supernatural "muscle" by means of which a person's transcendent self or soul overcomes her strongest desire in favor of a weaker but morally preferable desire.[8] This introduction of a supernatural source of energy to explain moral effort takes too literally the analogy between muscular effort and moral effort and falls into what Gilbert Ryle aptly termed the "paramechanical" account of the will. It becomes vulnerable to the same objection that Campbell raised against naturalistic causal accounts of action by implying that what makes it possible for the sinner to reform is the possession of a supernatural power strong

enough to control one's natural desires. For if that is true, then it is
easy for sinners to reform and they do not deserve extra credit for
moral effort. What Campbell first perceptively noticed and then lost
sight of is that the role of the concept of moral effort is precisely to
indicate that the action was not predictable on the basis of *any* causal
factors, whether natural or supernatural. By regarding moral effort
as non-causal only in terms of natural processes but as causal in
terms of supernatural processes, Campbell falls into the same error
as the determinists he criticizes.

What then do we mean by "moral effort" and is there really such
a phenomenon, or is the term only a disguised way of admitting our
ignorance of the causal processes that led to an action that surprises
us? Determinists take the latter view and so do supernatural libertarians like Campbell. I suggest that the explanatory role of the
concept of moral effort is *neither* naturalistically nor supernatural-
istically causal. On the contrary, its role is precisely to indicate that
any kind of deterministic explanation is out of place in somewhat
the way that the response "I did it because I felt like it" indicates that
any demand for a reason is out of place.[9] Since any proposed deterministic explanation of an action implies that, if we knew all the
causal factors in advance, we could have predicted the action taken,
such an explanation undermines the ascription of moral effort by
showing it to be merely a confession of ignorance and cannot therefore justify the awarding of extra credit. So either "moral effort" is
a metaphor for unknown causal factors, in which case the elder son's
complaint that it does not deserve extra credit was well taken, or
"moral effort" signifies the objective unlikelihood (i.e., unlikelihood
even on the basis of adequate knowledge of all relevant antecedent
facts) of the victory of duty over inclination, and such likelihood is
a fair measure of the difficulty surmounted and the father's award of
extra credit to his prodigal son was wise and just. The latter account

seems to me the only way to make good ethical sense of the "pearl and crown" of the parables, and I need hardly point out that it entails an indeterministic view of psychological causality.

Moral Luck

B. A. O. Williams and Thomas Nagel, among others, have recently maintained that we are morally responsible for matters that are not at all, or very little, within the scope of our voluntary control as subject to our decisions, and they call this feature of moral life "moral luck." If they are right about moral luck, then my claim that degree of moral responsibility, to be fair, must be proportionate to degree of moral effort is mistaken. They have argued persuasively that we often judge ourselves and others as responsible for conse-quences of our actions over which we have no control or power of decision, for various reasons that Nagel classifies under three main headings: (1) character strengths and defects, (2) opportunities and challenges, and (3) accidental circumstances as when a child runs in front of one's car. Nagel rightly deplores the phrase "moral luck" as paradoxical, but he thinks the paradox is deep and inescapable.

Since it is a paradox, it seems to me that there is a heavy burden of proof on those like Williams and Nagel who deny that the paradox can be resolved. And I do not think they have shouldered that bur-den. Consider the three types delineated by Nagel:

1. Are we both lucky (or unlucky) and *also* morally responsible for our character traits? Lucky or unlucky, yes, but I think not morally so, in the sense of being responsible for them. I have argued that to be held responsible both for one's actions and for one's character is to be unfairly victimized by double jeopardy. Granting Nagel and Williams that we are, in fact, criticized for our character

defects, it is not self- evident that the criticism is moral criticism, rather than, say, aesthetic or prudential. It is bad to be cowardly, but if one is naturally timid so that it requires great effort to face danger, then one merits more credit for overcoming one's fear, and less discredit for failing to do so, than those who are naturally courageous. It would be terribly unfair to blame the coward for running away and then to blame him further for being cowardly, as Aristotle noted in distinguishing the true courage of the citizen from the pseudocourage of the professional soldier.

2. Is it true as Nagel claims that the citizens of Nazi- governed territories who collaborated with the Nazis are more reprehensible than those of other lands who were spared the necessity of choosing between collaboration with evil and resistance to evil? I don't think so. What is true is that we have stronger evidence of their character defects and so we are more inclined to judge them adversely. We have no right to condemn people on suspicion alone, since we can be so easily wrong in our estimates in advance of a person's actual conduct, so we withhold blame from those we merely suspect would be collaborators *if* they were subject to political and social pressures, but it doesn't follow that they are, in fact, less contemptible. It follows only that we don't know their degree of culpability and therefore we owe them the benefit of the doubt.

3. A similar alternative account can be applied to the third type of alleged moral luck, where accidental circumstances appear to make one person more responsible than another for the same action, as when a child runs in front of one drunken driver, who is then guilty of homicide, while another, luckier drunk arrives home without incident. The second drunk was, we say, lucky not to have killed anyone. But "lucky" here means prudentially fortunate, not morally so. I see no moral difference whatsoever between the two cases. The law punishes the unlucky driver more, and we ourselves feel more

remorse if we are that driver, but, again, this is for the sound reason that we cannot be sure, even in our own case, that the lucky driver, had she been faced with the emergency of the child running into the street, would not have had the presence of mind to stop the car in time or change direction skillfully. That is, we cannot be sure that she was too far gone to avoid disaster. And if the driver was, in fact, dead drunk, then the driver is culpable for driving while drunk but, on the other hand, the degree of culpability is somewhat lessened by the fact that a dead drunk person is no longer able to realize that he or she should not drive. In any event, the main point is that any difference between the drunk who kills the child and the luckier drunk who doesn't is not a difference of degree of moral culpability. At least it is incumbent on those who believe otherwise to prove it.

5

HEALING SICK SOULS

The Goal of Psychotherapy

I have been maintaining that psychological causality, unlike physical causality, is non-necessitating because it is irreducibly triadic, requiring the agent to decide to act on the reason that, in itself, is only the potential cause of the action. Any dyadic account, I have argued, would reduce the agent to a passive victim or beneficiary of the causal factors within and without. Obviously, this thesis would, if accepted, have an impact on the methodology of psychology, and on economics, anthropology, sociology, political science, and history, insofar as they employ psychological explanations of individual actions rather than statistical projections of group behavior. In the previous three chapters I tried to show that this indeterministic view is needed to make sense of moral evaluation. I shall now attempt to show that it is also needed to make good sense of psychological explanation insofar as it is directed toward therapeutic goals. It would require an extensive argument, far beyond my competence, to prove this thesis for all of psychology other than, perhaps, psychophysiology, concerned as it is with the physiological mechanisms employed in cognitive and motor activities (which I think is not so much psychology as applied physiology, somewhat as forensic medicine is not law, but medicine applied to legal problems). I shall not attempt so ambitious a task, but I shall limit this discussion of psychology to its therapeutic aspects.

The central issue I wish to consider is this: If therapeutic psychology is, as it is usually claimed to be, the knowledge of the mechanisms, whether psychic or somatic, whose malfunctioning causes socially unsatisfactory conduct, does this entail that satisfactory conduct is causally determined by well-functioning mechanisms, or does it leave satisfactory conduct free to be explained in the indeterministic way I have described? I want to argue the latter thesis. If I am right about this, an important corollary follows—namely, that psychotherapy has no more scientific warrant than the advice of any person experienced in giving advice such as clergy, teachers, or heads of large families. This consequence may strike devotees of psychotherapy as a *reductio ad absurdum* of my account of psychological causality, but I regard it as positive confirmation, in the light of H. J. Eysenck's statistical finding that the percentage of spontaneous recoveries from clinically diagnosed psychic malaise is the same as the percentage of success claimed by psychotherapists.[1] The indeterminism of psychological causality nicely explains this statistical finding, which should, on the other hand, be mind-boggling to determinists.

I have always disliked the term "psychotherapy," not because I question the value of helping people to resolve their inner conflicts, which is an admirable thing to do when done out of the goodness of one's heart, and thus free of charge, but because the pretense of professional expertise and the pseudo-medical ring of "therapy" imply psychological determinism. Like Thomas Szasz, I object to the association of soul-healing with somatic medicine and, more consistently, I think, than Szasz, my reason is that medicine is properly deterministic, while soul-healing is not. If the mind or soul were the brain or its activity, then psychotherapy would be neurology, but in that case, the term psychotherapy is misleadingly redundant. I have no quarrel with clinical neurology, but we can set it aside as irrelevant. I shall argue against mind-brain reduction is the final chapter. At this point I want to consider what is wrong in the notion of (irreducibly) mental psychotherapy. I want to consider the claim that psychotherapy helps or benefits the person who avails himself of its services. To put my cards on the table, I shall say straight out that I cannot see how such a thing is possible. This is not because I hold any animus against psychotherapy or those who practice it. Some of my best friends are therapists and others of my best friends go to therapists and sometimes seem to benefit from doing so. I know at least three persons who attempted suicide and then, after receiving therapy, got along well enough not to have attempted suicide again—so far, at least. I know one young man who was shy and homosexual before therapy. After therapy he was boisterous and aggressively heterosexual. He ceased to write poetry, became an advertising executive and made lots of money. Perhaps these people did benefit from psychotherapy, at least from their point of view. But the question in my mind is not whether people do sometimes as a matter of fact derive benefit from psychotherapy, for I have no doubt that they do. People also sometimes benefit from prayer, transcendental meditation, faith healing, and even from catastrophe, if they are resourceful enough to draw the right lessons. The question I mean to explore is whether it is of the *nature* of psychotherapy that it benefits people, or whether whatever benefit one derives from it is accidental—that is, due more to surrounding circumstances than to the nature of the service performed, in the way that having an auto collision may shock a reckless driver into driving more carefully, or being swindled may teach a person to be less gullible, or in the way that Father Zossimov, in *The Brothers Karamazov*, during a night of anguish while preparing for a duel, experienced a religious conversion and became a saint. Lots of things benefit us in mysterious and accidental ways. But the kind of skill whose *nature* it is to provide benefit would be a practical science like automobile mechanics or agronomy or medicine. The automobile mechanic, if he is a good one, can be relied upon to benefit you by repairing your car. The agronomist can show you or tell you how to cultivate the soil so as to improve your tomato crop. The doctor can usually be relied upon to repair your body. What about the psychotherapist? What knowledge has she in virtue of which she can repair something for you or tell you how to repair it yourself? And what object of yours does she or you repair?

Some would say the object of therapeutic repair is the soul, others would say it is the mind, still others would say it is the self, and all would say that it is by repairing, that is, restoring to full efficiency, the soul, mind, or self that psychotherapy provides benefit in virtue of its nature, rather than by accident. But these are strange objects of repair—soul, mind, and self. I know nothing about my soul, nor about anyone's soul—not even if there is such a thing. As for my self, I think I know it well and I have no doubt that there is such a thing as self-improvement, but what this would seem to mean is education and that is hardly what psychotherapy provides. The usual conception of psychotherapy is that it is mental doctoring, the curing of mental illness or injury. But is the mind an entity, like the body, that you can bring to a doctor to be healed, restored, or repaired? If so, then who is the person—the you—who brings your mind to the therapist, like your car to the mechanic or your body to the physician? Gilbert Ryle, in *The Concept of Mind*, argued that the mind is not an entity that can be inspected, fluoroscoped, X-rayed, and repaired. It is, he claimed, a family of adaptive tendencies and skills, and the way to change or improve one's skills is by study and practice, not by having someone tinker with a ghostly organ inside one's skull.[2] In brief, one's mind is indistinguishable from oneself, and the only way, as I have already noted, to improve oneself is to learn. And it is the person who learns, not the therapist who improves or repairs the person. One may, of course, learn something from the therapist, and one may also learn something from an earthquake. But is the therapist a teacher? If so, what skill or kind of knowledge does she teach?

It may be said that one goes to a therapist to improve oneself, not in the sense of learning new skills but in the sense of becoming a better person. But then we may ask, in what way better? Does this mean better in the eyes of others or in one's own eyes? If better in the eyes of others, then one wants not really to become better but to make more friends and influence more people, like presidential candidates hiring make-up artists and public relations experts to make them look better than they really are. That surely is not the benefit that therapy should be expected to provide. If better in one's own eyes, does this mean happier or more virtuous? If happier, how can one become happier except by getting what one wants most in life, and how can one get what one wants except by learning and exercising various skills? If one wants power, one learns politics. Again, the question becomes what specific skill does the psychotherapist teach her patient? If better means more virtuous, then, as Socrates demanded of Protagoras, how on earth can one person make another more virtuous?[3] If anything is voluntary, virtue would seem to be. The way to become more virtuous is by performing virtuous acts, as Aristotle pointed out.[4] I am not asking these annoying questions just to be unpleasant any more than Socrates asked them just to be unpleasant. Socrates exposed the sophists because he considered it immodest for anyone to claim to have something called wisdom that she can sell to another. Wisdom, Socrates realized, is not a commodity. There is, let us hope, such a thing as wisdom but none of us should claim that we know just what it is and how it can be transferred from one person to another.

My reason for asking these questions is not quite the same as Socrates' reason, so far as I can see, although perhaps, on a deeper analysis, it might turn out to be the same. My reason has to do with personal dignity. It seems to me incompatible with the dignity of a person to expect to be made a better person by someone else, or even to expect to be assisted in becoming a better person. I think, for example, of Charles Colson joining an evangelical church in order to be reborn as a different and better person than the scoundrel who perpetrated the Watergate capers. One wonders which Charles Colson joined the church before he was reborn, the good one or the bad one. This search for a better self seems to me the ultimate in logical absurdity; it was rightly condemned by Sartre as an attempt to escape responsibility for one's actions.[5] To hope to be made a better person or even to be assisted in becoming a better person is to pretend that one has higher standards of conduct than one in fact has—to pretend, that is, that one wishes to be tinkered with by a mechanic of the soul so as to be made to conform to one's "true" standards, while also confessing that, without such tinkering, one would not live up to those standards. It is to pretend that one's soul or mind or self, like one's body and one's car, is a mechanism that can break down or malfunction and fail to do what one really wants it to do until it is repaired by the appropriate mechanic. But if one's soul or mind or self is such a mechanism, then who is the person who owns and operates that mechanism? The person would seem to be, if I may put a gloss on Gilbert Ryle, a ghost inside the ghost in the machine.

What I mean by personal dignity is that one behaves as befits a person, and not an automaton. To behave as befits a person is to accept responsibility for one's actions rather than blaming them on forces beyond one's control. And to conduct oneself with dignity is to insist on one's rights as a person, including the right of privacy. My thoughts, feelings, and desires are private. No one else can know them unless I choose to express them. To believe that we can have unconscious thoughts, feelings, and desires that another person can know better than we ourselves is to deny the epistemic authority that makes us persons and to pretend to be automata whose internal wiring can be inspected and repaired by a mechanic of the mind. Thus my reason for wanting to expose the incoherence in the concept of a science of psychotherapy is that I consider it to entail the denial of personal dignity and I fear that its growing influence is a serious threat to the continued recognition of the rights and responsibilities of persons on which democracy depends.

So far I have only explained why I intend to argue that the belief in the efficacy of psychotherapy is incompatible with the concept of a person. If I succeed in proving this, then I will have explained why it is so difficult to explain what kind of benefit a person can reliably expect to get from psychotherapy. The difficulty is due to the fact that, from the standpoint of psychotherapy, either there are no persons to benefit from anything, or else there is no specific benefit that psychotherapy can provide. These are my claims and now to my argument.

Four Models of Psychotherapy

I take it as non-controversial that the concept of a person entails the ability to perform some actions for which one can be held responsible. I also take it that responsibility for an effect entails responsibility for its cause, and non- responsibility for the cause of an effect entails non-responsibility for the effect itself. More technically, responsibility is ancestrally transitive along natural causal chains and non-responsibility is hereditarily transitive along natural causal chains. Now it follows from the principle of ancestral transitivity of responsibility and hereditary transitivity of non-responsibility that a person cannot be responsible for any link in a natural causal chain unless he or she initiated that chain. This is not to deny that a person can be held responsible for failing to *interrupt* a causal chain that he or she did not initiate—for example, a switchman who sees that two trains are about to collide and fails to switch them to different tracks. But to interrupt a causal chain is to initiate a new causal chain and to fail to do so is an omission for which one is responsible only if that omission is not itself an intermediary link in a causal chain that one did not initiate—as, for example, if terrorists who want the trains to collide distract the switchman or tie him up so that he cannot prevent the collision. It follows that if there is any such thing as moral responsibility, then there must be causal chains that we initiate or fail to initiate and that are not therefore segments of longer and perhaps more infinite causal chains. As the ancients put it, our actions must sometimes be first causes.

Now insofar as psychiatric theory assumes that the neurotic's actions are due to mental causes that in turn are due to more antecedent causes such as childhood traumas, parental misrearing, congenital defects, and/or pernicious environmental conditioning, it is in effect holding that our actions are intermediate links in natural causal chains extending back in time, perhaps infinitely, but at least prior to the very existence of the agent. On such a view, one's actions cannot possibly be events for which one has moral responsibility since they do not constitute first links of causal chains that one can be said to have initiated. A person can hardly be held responsible for events occurring prior to his or her very existence that are believed to have led causally to his present actions. Therefore, by the principle of heredity of non-responsibility along causal chains, one cannot be held responsible for one's present actions nor indeed for any of the events along chains that extend backward in time before one's maturity. It follows that no one is responsible for anything he or she does and if, as I have claimed, it is essential to the concept of a person that one can be held morally responsible for at least some of one's actions, then it follows that either there are no persons at all or that those who can benefit from psychotherapy are not persons.

Psychotherapeutic theorists who have sensed this difficulty have offered several solutions to it. The usual line of escape is the soft determinist line, which holds that there are two kinds of actions, neurotic and rational, or sick and healthy, and that one is morally responsible only for one's rational or healthy actions. No one, the argument goes, is totally neurotic; everyone acts rationally on some occasions. Neurotics are not non-persons or automata but incomplete persons who need assistance to extinguish those of their action-patterns that are traceable to remote causes in their childhood and beyond, and for these neurotic action-patterns they are not responsible. But they are still partially persons insofar so they are responsible for those of their actions that are explainable by rational causes consisting in conscious intentions, decisions, and purposes. Freud seems to have held this view when he proclaimed, "Where id was, let ego be," meaning that we should try to overcome the irrational unconscious causes of our actions so as to be free to obey the conscious, rational "causes" that constitute our egos. This creates the problem of explaining how it can make sense to divide *causes*, which are events, into rational and irrational events, or even into conscious and unconscious events. But the really hopeless problem is that this distinction is of no help whatsoever in escaping the dilemma of non-responsibility that it was designed to escape. If so-called rational causes such as conscious intentions, beliefs, purposes, and decisions are intermediate links in indefinitely extended causal chains, then on the principle of heredity of non-responsibility, we are no more responsible for our rational actions than for our neurotic actions. Recognition of this problem has led some theorists to propose a different line of escape as follows:

Only neurotic actions, they say, are links in indefinitely long causal chains. For these actions, we are not responsible, because we need the repair services of therapists to help us interrupt such causal chains by initiating new chains. However, our rational actions are what we do freely and responsibly; they are first causes in that they initiate causal chains and are not traceable to previous causes. The doctrine of determinism, on this view, is true only for pathological behavior while libertarianism is true for rational behavior. This position, which is taken by Philip Rieff in his book *Freud: The Mind of the Moralist,*[6] and by Erich Fromm and many others, has the merit of recognizing that we are persons endowed with free will and capable of acting with moral responsibility. But, it maintains, and with considerable plausibility, that we are not *always* free and responsible; we are not always full-fledged persons. The function of psychotherapy is to assist us to realize more fully our personal autonomy.

Plausible though it may seem at first glance, this view cannot be coherently sustained. How can some mental states be necessary effects of antecedent causes and others not? How can determinism be true of part of the mind and libertarianism be true of another part? The therapist of this eclectic persuasion employs the following criterion for judging whether some aspect of the patient's behavior is free or determined, voluntary or compulsive, rational or irrational: If the patient says she doesn't like what she is doing and doesn't want to do it, her behavior is neurotic and we should look for its causes. Otherwise, she is free and responsible. But what if the agent is deceiving herself or others in claiming that she does or doesn't really want to do what she is doing? In that case, says the therapist, we can tell from inconsistencies in her behavior and from vacillations, hesitations, signs of guilt or shame, that her reports of her real feeling and desires are not to be trusted.

This neat compromise between determinism and voluntarism has been formulated very clearly by Joseph Margolis in *Psychotherapy and Morality*, a book designed to defend psychotherapy against the charge that it eliminates moral responsibility. Margolis concedes that responsible action and causal determinism are incompatible but claims there is a place for both:

> The kinds of reasons that support the claim of someone's having acted deliberately preclude . . . the provision of causal determinants. The relevant reasons will be given in motivational terms—purposes in mind, alternative means, deliberations of strategy, decisions. . . . No one will deny that causal factors are relevant; for instance, the body must be adjusted to certain appropriate physical and chemical ways. . . . But to insist on a causal explanation of a man's behavior . . . is to *deny* that he acted freely and to assert that he was impelled by forces over which he has no control. . . . To insist on a causal explanation of some human action that has already been satisfactorily explained in motivational terms belonging to choice and decision is, quite simply, to misuse language . . . .[7]

> "Free" and "cause," therefore, serve in the context of explaining action as paired and opposing concepts: the sense of the one is fixed by its contrast with the other. . . .[8]

All of this should serve . . . to clarify the concepts of health and illness. The core of illness is victimization: one is, in a sense, struck down by forces over which he has no control. This is as true for viral infections as it is for paranoia. To say that someone is "mentally ill" is therefore to say that his condition is, in some sense, *caused* rather than chosen.[9]

The theorist of this persuasion is claiming that our neurotic desires are less really *ours* than our rational desires. We are, as Margolis puts it, "struck down" or overcome by them as by a viral infection, and they can be defeated only by assistance from a therapist since they are beyond our control. Now this claim can be interpreted in two ways: (1) Neurotic actions, like the berserk spasms of psychomotor epilepsy or like the sneezes and coughs produced by a cold, are not really human actions at all, but convulsions of the body due to some pathological condition. Or (2) neurotic actions are genuine actions motivated by genuine desires and intentions and purposes, but they are not within our control because they are not *our* desires, intentions, and purposes, but the desires, intentions, and purposes of alien persons inside us. The first interpretation seems to be the one suggested in the passage I have quoted from Margolis, but it would be unacceptable to Freud and to most therapists for good reason: It would reduce psychotherapy to ordinary somatic medicine. The distinctive feature of psychotherapy, which makes it *psycho* rather than *somatic* therapy, is that it is supposed to deal with and cure states of mind such as neurotic desires, purposes, and intentions, not states of the body such as viral infections and seizures. Thus, if psychotherapy is not to be reduced to somatic medicine, it must insist on the second interpretation.

But the second interpretation, that neurotic desires and intentions are the work of an alien person inside the patient, involves the desperate device of splitting a person into two or more persons, and revives the ancient superstition of demoniacal possession, which it makes more palatable only by camouflaging it with the pseudo-scientific terminology of psychodynamic causality. For if the unconscious forces controlling us are genuine desires, they must be the desires of some person, and if the person is not oneself, then it must be an alien person inhabiting one's body. Thus we seem to get the best of both worlds, the religious world of demoniacal versus angelic persons, and the scientific world of psychodynamic causal processes. The only trouble, but it is a big trouble, is that the two worlds won't mix. If my neurotic desires are genuine desires, and they are not really mine, then they are the desires of a demon. On the other hand, if they are mere psychodynamic forces, then they are not desires at all, and they cannot be said to motivate specific actions. (Forces, as Margolis points out, don't *motivate,* they only cause.) Thus, in the guise of combining determinism with free will by claiming that neurotic actions are intermediate links in extended causal chains, while granting that rational actions initiate causal chains, theorists, like Margolis are really suggesting that neurotic actions are initiations of causal chains after all, not by the patient, but rather by a demonic pseudo-self inside him. For if neurotic actions were not initiations of causal chains by some agent, they would not be actions at all, and if they were not motivated by the desires of some agent, they would not be motivated at all; they would be spasms, not motivated actions. So much for the doctrine of mental illness. One might object, but what about compulsive behavior like kleptomania? Isn't there clearly such a phenomenon, and isn't it a case of genuine action that is clearly not really desired by the agent? To that objection my answer would be that a compulsive action is not one that the agent does not want to perform, nor is it a spasm, nor is it what another agent inside him wants; rather, it is something the agent both wants to do and disapproves of doing, so that he has conflicting desires and intentions. Perhaps it would be so painful for the kleptomaniac to desist from stealing that we can hardly expect him to be all that stoical and heroic. Nevertheless, if he steals because it would extremely frustrating for him not to do so, then clearly he is acting on a genuine desire to avoid intense suffering, and that desire is his own, not a psychodynamic force that overcomes him like a virus, and not a desire of some demoniacal pseudo-self.

The final move to escape the dilemma of responsibility has been made by existential psychotherapists like R. D. Laing[10] and Rollo May,[11] phenomenological psychotherapists like J. H. van den Berg,[12] and educational psychotherapists like Albert Ellis,[13] Thomas Szasz,[14] E. F. Torrey,[15] and Roy Schafer.[16] They maintain that we are always free, whether we are neurotic or rational, and that the task of psychotherapy is not to repair our psychic mechanism but to advise us and train us to act more prudently and more effectively. They reject the medical model for psychotherapy and propose to replace it by an education model. The therapist no longer appears as a mechanic or gardener or doctor of the mind, but as a moralist and a teacher. This view is at least to be commended for restoring the dignity and autonomy of the person. The only fault I find in it, which is not a grievous fault from my standpoint but must surely be grievous from the standpoint of professional psychotherapists, is that it undermines the claim that psychotherapy can by its very nature provide specific benefits and it makes whatever benefit the patient happens to derive rather fortuitous, like the benefit one sometimes gets from conversation with a friend or, for that matter, with a stranger on a train. For, as Socrates demanded of Protagoras, we may ask of the therapist: If you are a teacher, what skill do you teach? There is no single general skill involved in being virtuous or in becoming happier, but only various specific skills in employing effective means to achieve specific ends. The riding master teaches us to ride better, the elocution teacher to speak better, the logician to reason better. What particular skill does the therapist have mastery in which she can impart to us? Presumably, a little of each. She is a college curriculum all in one. That is exactly what the sophists were: one-man colleges. But we have come a long way since the time of Protagoras, and there is far too much to know for one person to master it all. Wouldn't it make more sense to go back to school and avail oneself of proven expertise in each specific skill or problem-solving method than to resort to psychotherapy?

I must repeat that I am not denying that psychotherapy can be of benefit to some people sometimes. I am only maintaining that there is no specific benefit that follows from the nature of the discipline in the way that specific benefits follow from the nature of automobile mechanics or medicine, because for specific benefits to follow from a discipline it must be in possession of causal laws, such that removal of a cause ensures removal of its undesireable effects. That is what is involved in repairing a defective mechanism, whether organic, as in gardening and medicine, or inorganic as in mechanics. Now I think I have shown that if there were such laws of human psychology, then we would not be persons. It follows that only non-persons can benefit from the nature of psychotherapy.

Margolis' Defense

In a reply to the above critique of psychotherapy published in the *Journal of Psychoanalysis and Scientific Thought*, Professor Margolis pinpoints the nub of my argument in my principle of heredity of non-responsibility along deterministic causal chains. I proposed that if an agent is not responsible for a cause, he or she is not responsible for its effect. (For brevity, I shall refer to this principle as T-R.) I then argued that any determinist account of the nature of psychotherapy, when conjoined with T-R, entails that, since every causal chain extends backward indefinitely in time, no one ever initiates such a chain and therefore no one is ever morally responsible for anything.

Margolis rejects T-R as "plainly false," on the grounds that one person may sometimes be held "criminally liable or legally responsible" for what another person initiated. He offers, as counterexamples to T-R, the responsibility of parents for their children's misdeeds, the liability of descendants for their progenitors' debts, and the strict liability of employers for the negligence of their employees. He concludes from these examples that I have "conflated being responsible, in the sense of being the causal agency of, with being responsible, in the sense of being legally or morally held responsible."

The sin of conflation is not mine. T-R was asserted to apply to moral, not legal, responsibility. Margolis' examples are drawn mainly from areas of legal responsibility and liability, areas that sometimes overlap with, but should not be confused with, moral responsibility. The strict liability of an employer for the negligence of an employee, or of a parent for the damages wrought by her child, or of an heir for the debts of the legator, has nothing to do with moral responsibility. It is, with respect to my argument, a red herring.

The responsibility of parents for their children is, of course, both moral and legal, and under the latter, we can distinguish two subtypes: civil liability and criminal negligence. Parents may be civilly liable for damage caused by their children. This is strict liability, which has no more to do with moral responsibility than has no-fault insurance. Parents may also be held criminally negligent, both legally and morally, if they corrupt their children, or fail to maintain minimum surveillance so as to prevent serious mischief. But even this is not the sense of responsibility that is relevant to my argument. For even here, parents are not guilty of the actions or causal chains initiated by their children. If the parent, in some Svengali-like manner, or by coercion, made the child commit a crime, then it was the parent, not the child, who initiated the causal chain leading to the criminal harm. But if a child commits a theft or a murder, no matter how negligent the parent, the latter cannot justly be branded a thief or a murderer. There is after all a reasonable limit to the extent to which we can identify the actions, even of a small child, as not the child's actions after all, but the parent's. Parents are at most (coercion aside) responsible for something quite different from their children's actions, namely, for failing to fulfill the minimal parental duties of care and education and thus for the crime, if it be one, of parental negligence. Thus it is not the case that one person can be reasonably held morally responsible for an action (i.e., the initiation of a causal chain) by another person, even where the former is the parent of the latter.

I am gratified that Margolis accepted my definition of voluntary action as the initiation of a causal chain. For, aside from the problem just considered of transferring responsibility, once he conceded that agents initiate causal chains he thereby ruled out all deterministic accounts of voluntary action. By accepting the characterization of a voluntary action as a first cause, he undermined his claim that reasons are a species of natural causes in the sense that rational action admits of deterministic causal explanation.

I think Margolis was led into confusing moral with legal responsibility by his extreme conventionalism. In the passage quoted above, he speaks of "legal or moral responsibility" as if they were identical and, worse yet, he identifies being responsible with being held responsible. Later, he asserts that " 'responsible' . . . signifies a certain status, however assigned to particular agents relative to certain societal norms, that entails nothing about their causal roles or causal agency." Margolis makes it appear as if the assignment of moral responsibility were entirely a matter of social decision. Now such a view is far too relativistic. Ancient societies that punished animals and small children severely, and punished descendants "even unto the fourth generations" for the sins of their ancestors, were so lacking in moral understanding as to be fairly called barbaric. Assignment of moral responsibility to agents that, as Margolis puts it, "entails nothing about their causal roles or causal agency" would be, I submit, a lapse into barbarism, as when the Nazis exterminated the entire town of Lidice as punishment for the assassination of the local gauleiter. There may well be a conventional element in the assignment of some types of responsibility, as was already noted with respect to strict liability in civil law, but to suggest that moral responsibility is "relative to certain societal norms" and that to be responsible is the same as being held responsible implies that no distinction can be made between just and unjust, civilized and barbaric, procedures of blame and punishment.

It is surprising to me that Margolis directs so much firepower at T-R since I distinguished four different models for explaining the benefits of psychotherapy, and I employed T-R directly only in criticizing the first two. Margolis associates himself with my fourth model, the education model of Szasz, Laing, Schafer, et al. (although his earlier book, *Psychotherapy and Morality,* seemed to me to support the third model). My criticism of the education model was based on a different argument, one that Margolis simply disregards. He speaks blithely of "the use of professional skills to increase or assist in increasing the range of an agent's competence." My criticism of the education model was that I fail to see what specific skills are either employed by the therapist or transferred to the patient. I suggested that specific skills are learned in schools, from teachers who are proven masters of those skills, and I expressed doubt that there is a general skill of the kind Plato called the "art of living," which he identified with philosophical wisdom, a general skill that can be claimed either to be possessed by oneself or to be taught to others. Socrates denied the right of the sophists to claim to have wisdom and to be able to teach it to others. Whatever wisdom is, I doubt that it is a skill, and I agree with Socrates that any claim to have it and to teach it should be regarded with suspicion. The wisest people seem to be those, like Socrates, who do not make such claims. Nor do I mean to deny that we can and often do help each other to find our way through emotional crises and moral conflicts, but I do deny that there is, or ever will be, a scientifically warranted method for doing so. Here my difference with Margolis is in our degrees of confidence in the clarity and power of psychoanalytic theory and practice, rather than any sharp disagreement over facts. But I remain convinced that the vagueness of the therapist's claim to offer "professional assistance" calls for as much skepticism as the claim of the evangelist to offer assistance toward salvation. Neither the alleged benefit nor the method of warranting it seems clear enough to justify submitting oneself to spiritual doctoring.

6

THE MYTH OF MENTAL SCIENCE

Szasz' Palace Coup

The trial in 1976 of Patty Hearst for bank robbery dramatized the unresolved conflict between the two philosophical views of mankind we have been examining—namely, libertarianism and mechanism. Although armies of eminent psychiatrists, armed to the teeth with degrees, honors, government grants, and proofs of expertise, testifying with equally dogmatic certainty on both sides, have become an all too familiar sight, a special feature of that trial was that the defense claimed innocence on the grounds of a newly baptized mental illness called "coercive persuasion" by the experts and "brainwashing" by the layman.[1] The question raised by that trial was whether there is such an illness as brainwashing, and, more generally, whether there is any such thing as mental illness. Some psychiatrists, led by Dr. Thomas Szasz, say no. So, apparently, did the Hearst jury. Almost three decades have passed since Thomas Szasz' heretical manifesto, *The Myth of Mental Illness,* burst among the devotees of psychiatric medicine, denouncing their idol as a fraud.[2] Yet today psychiatry and psychoanalysis are still thriving enterprises. I think the main reason for the failure of his campaign against medical psychiatry is that it was insufficiently radical. He attempted merely a palace coup instead of the full-scale revolution that is needed. Like that earlier heretic, Martin Luther, he replaced one dogma with another. Other psychiatric heretics, such as R. D. Laing and E. F. Torrey, have unfortunately followed suit.[3] Szasz' critique of medical psychiatry consists of four main theses that he regards as mutually supporting although, in fact, they are inconsistent: (1) The Myth: Mental illness is a myth like witchcraft and demonic possession. (2) Anti-Paternalism: Those who are forcibly treated for mental illness are cruelly and unjustly deprived of their rights. (3) Full Responsibility: People who deviate radically from conventional standards of conduct should not be relieved of full responsibility for their actions. (4) Psychotherapy as Social Science: Since there is no such thing as mental illness but only deviant behavior, psychotherapy should not be classified as a branch of medicine, but as applied social science or behavioral engineering. I shall argue that thesis (1), while true, is given an exaggerated importance, (2) is not only false, but inconsistent with (1), and (3) and (4) are half-truths whose partial falsity is more misleading than their partial truth is illuminating.

1. The Myth. Both Szasz and Torrey argue that bizarre behavior, such as delusory beliefs, sexual perversions, hysteria, and compulsions are wrongly considered symptoms of mental illness, on the grounds that our identification of abnormal behavior is dependent on variable social standards of normality, while bodily abnormalities are objectively identifiable in a fairly value- neutral way. Szasz admits that the concepts of health and illness are themselves normative concepts, but he holds that the criteria of bodily health, unlike those of mental health, are reasonably invariant. He concludes that "psychiatry . . . is very much more intimately tied to problems of ethics than is medicine. . . . What people now call mental illnesses are for the most part communications expressing unacceptable ideas."[4]

There is considerable justice in this complaint. The alarming variation in standards of behavioral normality has produced abominations such as the commitment to asylums and even the lobotomizing of critics of the Soviet government, including Jews who applied for emigration to Israel, and in the West, the classification of homosexuality and masturbation as emotional disturbances or behavioral disorders. Szasz, Laing, Torrey, and other critics have done a great service in bringing public attention to these abuses of psychiatric power and prestige, warning us against excessive trust in psychiatric expertise. But surely there is also some degree of relativity in our criteria of bodily abnormality. Is sexual impotence an illness or not? Those who take monkey gland treatments think it is, while those who take a vow of celibacy regard lust as the pathological state. And what of muscular flabbiness, or obesity, or suntan or mottled teeth or cleft palate? Whether these conditions are considered normal or abnormal depends on social and individual values, and one can find cultures or subcultures that regard them as ideal states, devoutly to be desired. Szasz himself observes, in *The Manufacture of Madness,* that Benjamin Rush, the founder of American mental hospitals, considered black skin a disease due to hereditary leprosy.[5] It is noteworthy that Szasz cites this fact as evidence for the variability of standards of *mental* illness although it really shows how wrong people can be about bodily illness. It must be granted that standards of behavior vary more widely than standards of bodily condition, but the difference is one of degree rather than kind and this seems insufficient to preclude reasonably objective judgments of radical abnormality. Few of us welcome delusions, although the recent mushrooming of religious cults and drug cults reminds us that even the distinction between delusion and veridical belief is not culturally invariant. On the other hand, we can find some cultures that prize scarification and other forms of bodily deformity. So the real ground for rejecting the concept of mental illness, if there is one, should not be sought in cultural invariance of standards. In my opinion, the real ground is to be found in the fact that human behavior is not fully determined by causal processes.

Evidence of a bodily disease consists of abnormal and generally undesirable states called "symptoms" such as high temperature, muscular weakness, changes of complexion, loss of appetite, and so on. These states are symptoms in that they are theoretically explainable as due to some known or unknown natural causal process that, if left unchecked, threatens to injure the agent and even shorten life. Now so-called mental and emotional disorders, such as delusions, compulsions, obsessions, and hysteria, would fit this definition of symptoms only if we had some well-confirmed theories of unobserved abnormal mental processes that produce them. But the trouble here is that we have no well-defined concept of a mental process of any kind analogous to a biochemical process such as bacterial infection or hormonal imbalance, nor have we any clear idea of a causal relation between the actions of a person and either a mental or a bodily process going on inside one. The reason for this is that human actions have only causally *necessary,* but not causally *insufficient,* conditions. The very idea of causally sufficient conditions for *voluntary* action seems self-contradictory. Bodily movements that are found to be fully explainable as results of internal causal processes, rather than explained as rational choices of the agent of means toward achieving her purposes, are thereby excluded from the class of voluntary actions. Natural causal processes can at most explain only an agent's ability or inability to perform an action. They cannot explain why she chose to perform one particular action rather than another.

Nevertheless, our tendency to describe abnormal behavior in terms borrowed from medicine is not entirely without rationale. When one finds oneself unable to follow a course of action one has set for oneself, when one feels in the grip of desires of which one disapproves but which one cannot control so that one suffers from frustration and self-hatred, when one calls out for help either explicitly or through such gestural expressions of hopelessness as schizophrenic withdrawal, it is irresistibly tempting to compare the condition with that of someone suffering from severe bodily illness. Perhaps the notion of mental illness is a metaphor that we often take too literally, but it seems so apt a metaphor that it is hard to get along without it. The same seems to me to be true about other phenomena of abnormal psychology, such as self-deception, weakness of will, phobias, and other forms of emotional or moral impotence. But the trouble with literally considering them as symptoms of a disease is that there seems to be no way of distinguishing the observable symptoms from the causal process that constitutes the alleged disease itself. The agent's behavior seems to have to do both jobs simultaneously unless, as psychiatrists are all too prone to do, we manufacture names of mythical causal processes, such as Freud's complexes and hypercathexes and "psychodynamics" of the unconscious. Once the human psyche is conceived of as a field of impersonal forces that determine the agent's actions, no ground remains for distinguishing voluntary behavior from compulsive behavior, and the theory of psychodynamic processes floats upward like a balloon that has broken free of its tielines.

An important fact that tends to be overlooked by both sides of the mental illness controversy is that an enormous range of behavior lies in a spectrum between the fully voluntary and the extremely compulsive, and that terms such as "weak-willed," "self-deceptive," "childish," "manic," "trance-like," "hypnotic suggestion," and "brainwashed" are rough and ready efforts to place behavior somewhere in this vague range. It seems to me folly to pretend that we can do so with anything approaching scientific exactitude, and Szasz and other critics of psychiatry was right to point this out. Nevertheless, until we can cash in our metaphors for a more literal account of such quasi-voluntary, quasi-non-voluntary behavior, the metaphor of illness provides us with a useful reminder that such persons are in need of assistance and are not fully responsible for what they do.

2. Anti-Paternalism. Is it an unjust invasion of the rights of the insane and the highly neurotic to compel them to undergo treatment? If it is unjust, the injustice cannot, I think, be blamed on the myth of mental illness, since an analogy to medicine in no way provides any argument for compulsory therapy. Patients in medical hospitals are not compelled to accept treatment, nor in any way relieved of responsibility for their conduct. Historically, the classification of psychotherapy as a branch of medicine was an enormous step forward in the humane treatment of the insane, who previously had been treated as dangerous criminals and were kept chained in dungeons. Szasz is therefore unfair to compare forcible commitment of the insane to the medieval burning of witches. The burning of witches was intended as punishment and was deliberately designed to cause suffering, whereas psychiatric treatment is aimed, whether successfully or not, at relieving distress and restoring the subject's freedom of action. Despite the abuses dramatized in such works as *One Flew Over the Cuckoo's Nest,*[6] abuses that unfortunately occur in any situation where some people have power over others (for example, child abuse), it seems to me unfair of Szasz to attribute these evils to the profession of medical psychiatry as if it were a police force commissioned to incarcerate and torture social deviants. This may indeed be the case in some communist countries, but if so, it is hardly the fault of the psychiatric profession.

Szasz, Laing, and Torrey claim that psychoses and neuroses are *merely* deviant modes of behavior motivated by unconventional beliefs and values.[7] Granted that in some cultures, and even some subcultures of our own such as religious cults, abnormal behavior is positively valued and rewarded, it does not follow that it is *merely* expressive of values different from our own. I once attended a conference on this topic at New York University, at which Dr. Szasz and other psychiatrists and philosophers condemned the myth of mental illness, whereupon various lunatics in the audience seized the microphones and shouted curses and obscenities at everyone, including Szasz himself. "Instead of just talking and making money," one fellow shouted at Szasz, "why don't you get your gun and shoot all those psychiatric fascists?" Dr. Szasz did not call the police, which on his own principles he should have done. Perhaps he had a momentary wish that some attendants from Bellevue had been there equipped with straitjackets. I know I had such a wish.

The point is that psychotic and neurotic behavior is not *merely* deviant or unconventional. It is deviant in a way that is not explainable by the agent herself in terms of her own values and rules of conduct. Usually the genuinely disturbed person has the same values and goals as those around her and suffers from the inability to pursue them successfully. She is not usually a radical, flouting society, and when she does play this role, as in the case of the Manson family or the SLA that kidnapped Patty Hearst, the glaring inconsistency of her actions with her avowed purposes and rules makes it clear that she is deceiving herself about her real motives, and we fall back on the inescapable metaphor: she is sick. Sometimes, she seems to us to be acting out a pretense that she has begun to take too seriously, like a small child playing wolf and becoming frightened. Some people have trouble distinguishing their role- playing from their real values. A good case in point is the former Yippy leader, Jerry Rubin, who wrote in 1976, in *Growing (Up) at Thirty-Seven:* "I found myself a victim of the media: people saw me as crazy,

95

dangerous, violent, insane. The image was driving me mad, until I realized that I believed it too."[8]

Does it follow that such people are not responsible for what they do and may be forcibly committed for therapy? That, I should think, depends on various factors and yields no simple answer. Do they indicate in their more normal moments that they want assistance, as do many who attempt suicide and then call for help? Is their behavior a serious danger to others? In the first case, the therapy is not really compulsory, while in the second case it is a necessary means of protecting others. Our society rightly places so high a value on individual liberty that compulsory measures are to be avoided if at all possible, and the subject should be given every reasonable benefit of the doubt. The practice of committing the allegedly insane on the authority of two psychiatrists is under legal attack and is in process of replacement by a more reliable legal process for which we can thank the efforts of critics like Dr. Szasz. But the excessive veneration for expert psychiatric opinion from which many have suffered is not due, as Szasz claims, to its employment of medical analogies. The high cost of medical malpractice insurance testifies to the fact that people are capable of recognizing medical incompetence. Our injustices toward the mentally and emotionally disturbed have their source in our disregard for the rights of anyone remote from our own small circle of acquaintance. They go with toleration of genocidal wars, racial discrimination, and police brutality, which is hardly due to being hung up on a medical model.

It is not merely the deviance of behavior, but our belief that compulsion, obsession, addiction, and delusion are self-injuring, contrary to the agent's own interests and impediments to his own long-range goals in life, that justifies some degree of paternalistic intervention and restriction of his freedom of action. Indeed, the types of explanation offered by Szasz and Torrey as alternatives to the medical model of mental illness are more supportive of paternalism than is the model they decry. Szasz accounts for hysteria as regression to an infantile pattern of helplessness, while Torrey explains self-injuring disorders as due to failure to learn more effective strategies of conduct. Now if a person is so infantile or stupid as to be in need of behavioral modification, then surely we have both a right and a duty to treat her paternalistically, as we treat infants and small children. The medical view that the patient is temporarily ill surely grants her more dignity and responsibility than the Szasz-Torrey view that, even at her best, she is incapable of more effective and intelligent behavior without the help of extensive retraining. Thus the alternative models of explanation offered by Szasz and Torrey seem inconsistent with their complaint that the medical model is offensive to individual autonomy.

3. Full Responsibility. Szasz and Torrey maintain that the concept of mental illness works to deprive eccentric people of responsibility for their actions. They seem to arrive at this conclusion from the consideration that insanity has been recognized as an excusing condition in criminal law. But they overlook the fact that it was not on *medical* grounds that insanity was accepted as exculpating an offender. The McNaghton rules specify mental derangement as defined in terms of ignorance of right and wrong or of the nature of one's acts. The efforts of psychiatrists, as reflected in the 1954 *Durham* case, to have all sorts of mental or emotional disorders accepted as excuses are quite another matter, and Szasz and Torrey are on firmer ground in opposing this tendency. Compulsions, obsessions, and hysteria belong to a quite different category of extenuating conditions than does derangement; they are more like coercion or duress in that they may reduce responsibility to some degree but do not eliminate it altogether. They indicate that the agent would have suffered by not performing the offensive action and thereby give us

some reason to reduce blame or punishment, but not to consider the agent innocent. The logic of excusing conditions is muddled in the minds of psychiatrists like Karl Menninger who claims that any kind of disorder entirely exculpates a person, but Szasz compounds this confusion by attacking the analogy to illness instead of arguing that illness does not rule out responsibility. Illness is a disability that can only explain and excuse the failure to perform a required action such as getting to work on time; it cannot explain why a successful action was so necessitated that the agent could not have refrained from performing it. There is no literal sense to the phrase "He could not stop himself from doing it." When we cannot literally stop ourselves, we are not *doing* anything, but undergoing something, such as slipping on a patch of ice. The concept of psychic compulsion is a useful metaphor, but a dangerous one in the wrong hands.

The Metaphor and the Myth

These considerations bring us to thesis 4 and the issue of whether psychiatry is a science and, if so, of what kind. Szasz and Torrey maintain that it is a branch of social science rather than a branch of biochemistry. Now the concept of social science has been assailed in recent years by a number of philosophers influenced by Ludwig Wittgestein who have argued that "science" entails well-confirmed causal theories and laws and that voluntary human actions cannot, on pain of conceptual incoherence, be explained by theories and laws. Whether or not this radical libertarian view is correct, the fact remains that there are as yet no causal generalizations about conduct worthy of the term "laws," nor well-confirmed theories about causal processes connecting antecedent bodily or mental events with subsequent behavior, that would enable us to predict specific human actions, such as passing the salt or writing a poem, independently of our knowledge of the agent's preferences and purposes. If my dinner companion asks me to pass the salt, you can predict that I will do so, not in virtue of your knowledge of some internal bodily or mental process that necessarily eventuates in salt-passing behavior, but in virtue of your confidence in my good manners. Should I happen to be harboring a grudge against my companion I might very well ignore her request, and should I misunderstand her words, I might pass the pepper instead. The point is that, in passing the salt, I am not obeying a law of nature over which I have no control; rather, I am following a rule and I have a choice whether to follow it or not.

Thus I think Szasz is wrong to stress the harm of the illness metaphor rather than the far greater harm of the belief, which he seems to share, in causal laws of human behavior. His proposal to shift from a medical model of psychotherapy to a "game-playing model" seems to me a leap from the frying pan into the fire, reminiscent of the pseudo-scientific jargon he deplores in medical psychiatry. What Szasz means by "game-playing" is not the field of mathematical logic developed by von Neumann, but common sense strategies for getting along with others and organizing one's life. Why then the pretentious title "game- playing model" if not to embellish mundane practical wisdom with the glamour of mathematical logic?

As if afflicted by pangs of conscience, both Szasz and Torrey apologetically explain their insistence on considering their discipline a science. In *The Ethics of Psychoanalysis,* Szasz writes, rather defensively: "It is only to be expected that psychoanalysts claim to be scientists. . . . The modern professional is compelled to make this claim for if his work were labelled nonscientific (or unscientific) he would be saddled with a value-negative identity."[9]

At this point in his discussion of ethics, Szasz seems to have confused ethics with public relations. Similarly Torrey, in *The Death of Psychiatry,* confesses with breathtaking candor: "To call something a science today is as much evaluative as it is an indication of methodology. Science means goodness, purity, efficiency, reliability, fidelity. . . . Everything claims to be based on science if it hopes to be accepted. This in itself is sufficient reason to call it 'behavioral science.' "[10]

The gnat of pseudo-medicine is strained at, but the camel of pseudo-science is swallowed. My suggestion is that we strain at both. Psychotherapy is at best a way of giving practical advice, involving experience, training, and personal insight, not a science applying causal laws. The myth that we need to free ourselves from is not that of mental illness, but that of causal determinism, the myth of an emperor whose transparent gown is woven of non-existent laws of human behavior.

7

YOUTH AND OTHER EXCUSES

Adolescence and Mental Illness

The punishment of juvenile crime raises the same problems as the punishment of adults said to be mentally ill. For every John Hinckley, who tried to assassinate President Reagan, and was judged not guilty on grounds of mental illness, there are thousands of teen-agers who stomp, stab, and shoot people due to much the same state of mind as Hinckley seems to have been in. In fact, setting aside the supposedly old-fashioned definition of insanity, that is, derangement or incapacity to know what one is doing and its consequences, the mental illness defense as formulated in the 1954 *Durham* decision would seem to apply as well to almost any juvenile crime as it does to crimes committed by mentally ill adults. What I have in mind as mental illness other than derangement (that state succinctly epitomized by Shakespeare as the inability to "tell a hawk from a hand-saw") is the entire grab bag of explanations of deviant behavior in terms of emotional disturbance, behavioral disorder, obsessional neuroses, compulsions, phobias, fixations, manic depression, and other such technical names for socially unacceptable patterns of conduct.[1] The point I want to make is that whatever measure of criminal responsibility we find it reasonable to apply to adults said to be mentally ill in this sense should apply *par excellence* to delinquent adolescents, for the reason that adolescence is by its very nature an emotionally disturbed, behaviorally disordered, obsessive, compulsive, phobic, fixated, and manic-depressive stage of life. Those youths who successfully navigate its turbulent waters without getting into serious trouble are either lucky or, as some psychologists have suggested, abnormally docile. It has been plausibly argued by Thomas Szasz, E. F. Torrey, and a few other psychiatrists that all psychopathology is due to arrested development; that is, a neurotic adult is a child who has failed to grow up, remaining fixated in an early pattern of responses to anxiety and frustration.[2]

I want to consider why it is that we hold the mentally ill less responsible for their actions than normal people. The term "mental illness" seems to me a metaphor that many people take too literally. Sometimes it is an apt and illuminating metaphor, but when employed carelessly, as it often is, it degenerates into a vague cliché that obscures rather than illuminates the problem of estimating degree of moral or criminal responsibility. The case of John Hinckley illustrates the deplorably widespread tendency to explain any bizarre pattern of conduct as due to something called mental illness" and as totally excusing criminal conduct.[3] For the last two decades, a small minority of psychiatrists led by Szasz, Torrey, and Laing have argued that the very concept of mental illness is a misleading metaphor, even a myth, on the grounds that the difference between physical health and illness is scientifically verifiable because it is value-neutral, while the difference between rational and irrational behavior depends on the standards of value and propriety dominant in a particular culture.[4] I think they are probably right about emotional disturbance but wrong about derangement, but I won't go into that here, because I want to raise a more fundamental question. Assume for the sake of the argument that there is literally such a thing as mental illness. *Why* does it reduce responsibility? No one to my knowledge has ever satisfactorily confronted this question, yet it fairly cries out for an answer. For consider: Mental illness is so-called on analogy with bodily illness. The resemblance is that both are undesirable states that reduce a person's ability to function effectively and thereby to live a long and satisfying life. Not every undesirable state of a person is an illness. Physical deformities and low intelligence are not so regarded. An undesirable state of mind or body is considered an illness only if it is abnormal for the individual as well as for the species, which is why lifelong defects are not ordinarily classed as illnesses. In any case, the point to bear in mind is that illness is at least partially definable as a temporary state that disables a person, insofar as it prevents her from doing many things she might want to do. Now disability ordinarily excuses failure to do what otherwise ought to be done, such as getting to work on time. It does not ordinarily excuse doing something that ought not to be done, such as committing a crime. One is not likely to be acquitted for robbing a bank or shooting a president on the ground that one was suffering from chicken pox. Why then should the appeal to mental illness excuse or even somewhat mitigate criminal conduct?

What I have said appears vulnerable to the objection that bodily illnesses sometimes produce in the sufferer intense needs whose satisfaction may require socially undesirable conduct. For example, a diabetic attack late at night might require that the sufferer, or someone acting for the sufferer, break into a drugstore to obtain the needed insulin, just as extreme hunger could drive an indigent person to steal food, and such acts of desperation are somewhat if not entirely excusable on grounds of overwhelming need. I would agree that great need is an excusing condition that mitigates blameworthiness, and I shall have more to say about this later. For the moment I merely wish to take note of the fact that cases where bodily illnesses engender needs that motivate one to perform immoral or criminal actions are rare and that, in such cases, the relevant excuse is not that the person is ill, but rather that she is driven by a need that happens to result from illness. Addictions are examples of need-engendering conditions that are not usually considered illnesses. So is intense fear, which is surely not an illness. A person in fear for her life may be excused for doing things, such as lying and stealing, for which she would otherwise be held to blame.

Yet when it comes to the plea of mental illness, the situation is paradoxically reversed. Mental illness is rarely cited as a disabling excuse for not doing what one normally should be doing, such as getting to work on time, but is also, and more frequently, held to constitute a causally sufficient condition for positively doing what one ought not to be doing, because it is believed to engender intense needs that demand immediate satisfaction although the only means of satisfying them involve committing a crime. Such compelling needs, or compulsions, are often taken as constituting in themselves a state of mental illness, rather than, as in the rare cases of bodily illnesses previously described, being engendered by some more fundamental abnormal state together with fortuitous circumstances that foreclose acceptable modes of satisfying them. Whether such compulsions are taken as illnesses in themselves or as symptoms of a deeper pathology depends on one's allegiance to a general psychiatric theory of their aetiology, and all such theories seem to me too speculative and controversial to support serious moral and legal judgments, so I shall limit my discussion to commonly identifiable patterns of behavior.

Two Kinds of Excuses: Derangement and Compulsion

Within these commonly identifiable patterns, it is important to distinguish two very different kinds of excuse on grounds of mental illness which the *Durham* decision, and people influenced by the *Durham* decision—for example, Judge Irving Kaufman as indicated in a *New York Times* article—neglect to distinguish, thereby contributing to the widespread confusion on how to estimate degrees of responsibility.[5] The two radically different grounds of excuses lumped together under the cliché of mental illness are: (1) derangement, or plain old-fashioned madness, encapsulated in the notorious and, I think, unfairly abused McNaghten rule (abused, for example, by Judge Kaufman in his article), and (2) practically all the emotional disturbances, behavioral disorders, obsessional neuroses, fixations, phobias, compulsions, and other abnormal mental states that people cite as excusing conditions for misbehavior. I take it that this distinction corresponds roughly to what psychiatrists call psychosis and neurosis, but this more technical terminology, which rests on speculative theories, seems to me less useful than the common sense distinction between being mentally deranged and being emotionally disturbed.

I think it important to consider separately, with respect to these two senses of "mental illness," the question of why and to what extent they mitigate moral and criminal responsibility.

Derangement seems to me a disabling state of the mind that is strikingly similar to the normal state of early childhood and also to that of severely retarded adults in that all three are states of extreme cognitive disability. The sufferer is unable to understand, in terms common to normal adults, what she is doing and why she should or should not be doing it. She lacks the reliable beliefs, the understanding of causal processes, and the lively sense of the needs and attitudes of other persons that are indispensable for forming rational plans of action. In brief, she is insufficiently rational to be held responsible for her conduct. It is not so much that her actions are bad but excusable, as that the entire language game of voluntary action and responsibility does not apply to her behavior any more than to that of an infant or an idiot. It is the duty of others to take care of her and, if possible, help her to acquire or re-acquire the cognitive abilities she has lost or not yet developed. Here there is no vexing difficulty in determining degree of responsibility. As with the small child, responsibility increases gradually with increase of cognitive ability, that is, with progress toward adult sanity.

There seems to be little controversy about derangement nullifying responsibility. The usual disputes concern the second type of so-called mental illness, and the reason why so much disagreement and confusion are engendered by this concept is, I think, the reason why Szasz and others reject the concept altogether—namely, because it does not satisfy the defining condition of illness that it be a disabling state. Alleged mental illnesses other than derangement do not prevent the sufferer from doing what he wants or should want to do, such as get to work on time, but rather seem to compel him to do what he doesn't or shouldn't want to do. They seem, that is, to necessitate positive actions that would, if normally motivated, be blameworthy but, if necessitated in this way, are partially or completely excusable. Now my question is: *why* does emotional disturbance or psychic compulsion reduce responsibility? The answer can hardly be the same as in the case of derangement since, as we have seen, derangement is a disability, whereas these states are not. Disability fully excuses for the reason formulated by Kant, but known intuitively to everyone, that "ought implies can"; that is, it would be unfair to blame a person for not doing what she cannot do. But in the case of this second and non-disabling type of mental illness, we are considering whether it is fair to blame a person for doing what she (or her psychiatrist) claims she cannot help doing, rather than for failing to do what she cannot do. And the very notion of not being able to help doing something—in a word, compulsion—is rather puzzling. Why should refraining or forbearing be beyond a person's power? It's usually easy not to do something, since it takes no physical effort, like falling off a log. It is true that we sometimes speak of forbearance as difficult, requiring considerable effort of the will rather than physical effort. When we do so speak it is when the agent is tempted to perform some improper action and tries, perhaps unsuccessfully, to resist the temptation. How do you suppose one can try to resist a temptation? One can try to *avoid* situations that might present temptations, and, should one find oneself willy-nilly already in such a situation, one might try to distract oneself, like the saint in a story of Tolstoy's who, on the verge of being seduced by a nymphet, whips out a knife and slices off his little finger. This conduct is, I think, not so much direct resistance to temptation as self-distraction from it. Directly resisting temptation requires effort of will, while distracting oneself renders such effort unnecessary. But the direct resistance to temptation that we call forbearance is, as Arthur Danto once rightly observed[6] (and then later wrongly repudiated),[7] a basic action, one that does not allow for a distinction between trying to do and doing, since there is nothing else one has to do to get it done; one simply does it. In the case of the negative basic action of forbearance, one simply forbears.

What then can we mean by saying that it is sometimes difficult to resist temptation, and thus difficult to forbear from doing what we know to be improper, such as overeating or taking that second cocktail before driving home? Since the only necessary condition for forbearance is the will to forbear, we must mean, not that the forbearance involves any obstacles the overcoming of which are necessary conditions for it, as we mean in the case of positive actions, but rather that it is difficult to *will*, or to continue to will, to forbear, like the soldier who at first wills not to give information under torture but finds his will weakening as the torture continues. Harry Frankfurt has analyzed this situation in the following way: The subject has a first-order desire to be relieved of his pain, and a second-order desire not to be relieved of it at the cost of giving military information. At first his second-order patriotic desire governs his will, but gradually his first-order desire to escape the pain becomes dominant.[8] This is a perfectly sound way of describing the matter but not, I think, the only nor the most illuminating way. The trouble with Frankfurt's account, like that of most determinists, is that it makes the agent appear to be a kind of passive spectator of warring forces within himself, playing no active part in deciding the outcome. I therefore propose the following, more libertarian account:

When the soldier is tempted to give information under torture, he wants to give the information, but disapproves of doing so and therefore wants also not to do it. As his desire to be relieved of the pain intensifies, his suffering, we say, becomes unbearable, and the temptation to give in becomes irresistible. But what do we mean by "unbearable" and "irresistible?" I suggest that we use these adjectives metaphorically, by comparing the suffering to an enormous boulder and the temptation to an oncoming locomotive, for these adjectives do not in this context indicate the absence of necessary conditions for forbearance, in the way that literal reference to a huge boulder or an oncoming locomotive would indicate the physical impossibility of carrying the boulder or of withstanding the locomotive. In short, what we mean is not that the soldier's suffering is literally unbearable and his temptation to give in literally irresistible (after all, some soldiers do endure and resist) but merely that they are *well nigh* unendurable and irresistible. And what do we mean by "well nigh?" I suggest that we mean simply that the one is as excusable as if it were the other; not bearing the pain is as excusable as not lifting an enormous boulder; giving in to temptation is as excusable (or well nigh so) as not withstanding an oncoming locomotive. In brief, the only common denominator between alleged psychic forces and literal physical forces is that both excuse moral failure. But while physical force explains moral failure as causally necessitated, psychic force explains nothing; it merely excuses, because it is a metaphor that determinists are "determined" to take literally.

I am not denying that "psychic compulsion" is often an apt metaphor, but merely insisting that in order to understand its role in mitigating responsibility we have to unpack it and identify its literal content. That is what I will now try to do, so as to draw some conclusions about the criminal responsibility of juvenile delinquents and other emotionally disturbed people.

Constraint Metaphors

Metaphors of constraint, such as "I had to do it," "I had no choice," "I was compelled by circumstances, by logic, or my responsibilities," "I was in the grip of an uncontrollable impulse," and so on, seem apt descriptions when the subject of them was in a state of intense conflict due to wanting incompatible things. The compulsive eater wants both to lose weight and to eat her fill. But mere conflict of desires is not yet a state of compulsion. As Harry Frankfurt has observed, the subject must also want *not to want* the object of her compulsive desire, and yet tend to act to satisfy that desire in the very teeth of her own disapproval. As Frankfurt analyzes the situation, the subject refuses to identify herself with the desire on which she acts, because that compulsive desire is contrary to her long-range goals and self-image. She feels that her shameful desire is somehow not really hers, but stems from an alien source as if she were possessed by a demon. The evidence for sincerity in feeling this way would consist in expressions of remorse for what one has done, one's efforts to avoid situations in which one is likely to repeat such actions, one's pleas for assistance from friends, relatives, and rabbi, and other such indications of genuine, rather than merely ceremonial or hypocritical, claims that one disapproves of what one has done.

Frankfurt holds, mistakenly in my opinion, that constraint descriptions apply with the same force even when a person approves of what he is doing, as when Luther in denouncing the church asserted "I can no other," and as a doctor might say to a doomed patient, "I am compelled by the X-ray evidence to inform you that you are dying of cancer." This use of constraint metaphors seems to me more a matter of ceremonial politeness, like saying, "Excuse me but I have to disagree with you," than a serious plea for excuse on the grounds that one really cannot help oneself, because one's will is in the grip of some alien power. This polite use of constraint language is more euphemistically metaphorical than its use in describing compulsive behavior, although both uses have the following feature in common: The agent in some manner dislikes or regrets what she is doing. In the case of Luther and the doctor, the agent regrets but, all things considered, approves of what she is doing, while in the case of a true compulsive, the reverse is true. Perhaps this is why we are so strongly tempted to think of "psychic compulsion" as a literal description rather than a mere metaphor. It has at least this much literal content, that when properly used it signifies a conflict between long-range goals and immediate impulse to do shameful or silly things such as steal, expose oneself, or periodically wash one's hands. This condition is sufficiently similar to bodily illness, in being undesirable to the agent and abnormal for her as well as for the species, to conclude, contrary to Szasz, that "mental illness," metaphor though it be, is often an illuminating description of a person's state.

I argued earlier that bodily illness does not excuse bad conduct, but only failure to perform up to expectation. On those rare occasions where bodily illness engenders an intense need whose satisfaction requires wrongful action, it is not the illness but the engendered need that excuses, and the importance of this distinction is that we measure the degree to which the need excuses by the intensity of the need. What is the measure of the intensity of the need? I suggest that the intensity or compellingness of a need can be measured by the amount of hardship and sacrifice that the subject is willing to undergo in order to satisfy the need, just as the intensity of one's disapproval of it is measurable by what one is willing to undergo to free oneself from its grip. If the subject is prepared to sacrifice anything, even life, to satisfy a need, then we can fairly judge that she is unable to forbear, and that her wrong action is fully excusable. This is the case when a soldier gives information under prolonged torture or a heroin addict suffering from extreme withdrawal symptoms steals in order to obtain the drug. Note that even these extreme cases are quite unlike the behavior of a deranged person, in that the compulsive is performing a rational action in adopting effective means to achieve an objectively recognizable goal, whereas the behavior of a deranged person cannot be so described. Thus it would be more accurate to say that the compulsive may be excused for his actions, while the madman performs no actions for which either blame *or* excuse would be appropriate. Consequently, exculpation by appeal to mental illness remains seriously ambiguous unless it is made clear which of these two radically different types, derangement or compulsion, is being alleged. For in the former case, there is no *mens rea*, no imputation of criminal intent that needs to be excused, while in the latter case there is such an intent, but it may be partially or entirely mitigated depending on the degree of intensity of the motivating need. In brief, psychic compulsion somewhat reduces, but does not render irrelevant, the ascription of responsibility.

Now what has all this to do with juvenile crime? I take it to be common knowledge that bodily and cognitive capacities develop more rapidly, at least in our culture, than the emotional stability or wisdom that comes only with full maturity. An adolescent, unlike a small child, usually knows enough about the social and physical consequences of conduct to satisfy the cognitive conditions of moral and criminal responsibility, but seldom has clearly defined long-range goals that motivate restraint of immediate desires, so that one's desires appear to one as needs just as compelling as that of the soldier under torture or the addict in need of a fix.[9] Granted that the adolescent's evaluation of needs is subjective; so is that of the compulsive. What makes the adolescent's need sometimes compelling, as in the compulsive's case, is that he or she is willing to sacrifice life, liberty, and the future pursuit of happiness in order to satisfy it. The only difference is that the adolescent does not value life, liberty, and future happiness as much as does the adult compulsive, which is why adolescents are not entrusted with grave responsibilities, such as piloting commercial airplanes, performing surgery, or governing a nation. But this very difference makes their conduct more, rather than less, excusable than that of compulsive adults, for they lack even more profoundly the clear self-image and plan of life essential to control their desires. Thus whatever degree of mercy and understanding society shows to the John Hinckleys and Patricia Hearsts who dominate our headlines, at least as much should be extended to the nameless juvenile delinquents of our urban and suburban slums. The general conclusion I wish to draw is that emotional disturbance, whether adolescent or adult, provides only a degree of mitigation of moral responsibility and not, like derangement, total nullification. A good deal of philosophical talk about "excusing conditions" tends to obscure the important difference between excuse as mitigation and excuse as nullification of responsibility.

8

WITTGENSTEIN'S CHALLENGE

The Challenge

There is an argument, first suggested by Wittgenstein, to the effect that causal explanation is inappropriate to the explanation of human action. Wittgenstein applied the argument only to psychology, but some of his followers, such as Peter Winch and A. R. Louch, have extended it to all the social sciences. To my knowledge, this argument has not been adequately faced by social scientists nor by their philosophical spokesmen.

In *The Blue Book,* Wittgenstein says:

> At this point another confusion sets in, that between reason and cause. One is led into this confusion by the ambiguous use of the word "why." . . . The proposition that your action has such and such a cause is a hypothesis. . . . [But] in order to know the reason which you had for making a certain statement, for acting in a particular way, etc., no number of agreeing experiences is necessary, and the statement of your experience is not a hypothesis. The difference between the grammars of "reason" and "cause" is quite similar to that between the grammars of "motive" and "cause."[1]

In *The Idea of a Social Science,* Peter Winch developed this distinction between cause and reason into an elaborate network of arguments for the thesis that human actions, whether individual or group actions, must be understood in terms of reasons, motives, and rules, entities that are conceptually, rather than empirically, related to the actions they explain. On the other hand, causal explanations such as are found in the natural sciences involve laws and theories that relate causes to effects, and these laws and theories must be subject to empirical confirmation, if not individually, at least at nodal points. Consequently, explanations of human action are not of the same type as causal explanations in the natural sciences. Talk of theory here is pretentious and misleading. Purported causal theories of human behavior are either disguised tautologies or pseudo-scientific fabrications.[2]

Philosophers who have attempted to refute this argument have not, to my knowledge, succeeded. If an adequate refutation were available, that is, if the Wittgensteinian argument were unsound, then it would be rather scandalous that no one has been able to expose the fallacy in it. My respect for the intellects of those who have tried and failed strengthens my conviction that the argument is sound and that no refutation is possible. I shall consider some representative counterarguments by Richard Rudner and David Braybrooke, showing how they miss their target and why further efforts in the same direction are unlikely to succeed.

The Wittgensteinian thesis is subject to easy misinterpretation, which may be the reason why attempted refutations of it have so far missed their target. Our first task, if we are to assess the issue fairly, must be to state the thesis in a precise and unambiguous form. Words like "science," "theory," "explanation," and "cause" are so notoriously ambiguous, so likely to be used in different senses by different writers and even by the same writer in different contexts, that our first task must be to disambiguate these terms. Let us take "science" in a tolerantly general sense to mean any kind of reasonably objective, careful, informed, and publicly confirmable inquiry. When Winch suggests that social inquiry must be philosophical or ethical rather than scientific, his use of "science" is unnecessarily narrow. There is no reason why ethical, philosophical, and even aesthetic studies should not be called scientific when they satisfy the standards of fairminded, careful, and informed inquiry. What Winch obviously means is that social inquiry cannot be causal in a deterministic (dyadic) sense of "cause." But to insist that deterministic explanation is essential to scientific inquiry seems unreasonably tendentious. The same can be said of the term "theory." What Winch, Louch, Richard Peters, and others mean by their claim that social inquiry has no need of theory is that a certain type of theory, namely, *deterministically explanatory* theory, has no place in such inquiry. Human actions are not subject to what William Dray calls "covering-law models"; they are not deducible from theoretical postulates together with antecedent conditions and causal laws. The Wittgenstein-Winch-Louch thesis should therefore be stated as follows: The construction of deterministic causal theories for deducing human actions from antecedent events together with laws is inappropriate to the explanation of individual and social behavior.

Critics of these writers justifiably take umbrage at the suggestion that all the hard work done by social scientists in gathering reliable data about societies, in subjecting the data to rigorous statistical analysis, and in constructing sophisticated formal rules for extrapolating from sample classes to whole populations, or from past regularities to future, that all this ingenious effort is misguided. Winch surely overstates his case in this respect, and Louch, for one, disavows such overstatement.[3] Let us therefore set aside the name-calling issue as to whether social inquiry can be "scientific," and focus our attention on the core problem, as to whether social inquiry can provide causal explanations in the narrow sense defined above.

The reasons offered by Winch, Peters, and Louch why social inquiry cannot be deterministically explanatory are that the explanation of human behavior is value-dependent and is culturally variant, while causal laws and theories are value- neutral and culturally invariant. It need hardly be argued that a causal law must be value-neutral. Whether copper does or does not melt at 325 degrees does not depend in any way on whether it is good or bad for it to do so. But an alleged "law" of human behavior, such as the generalization that a consumer will purchase a commodity at the lowest available price, obviously does depend very much on whether the consumer believes it is good or bad to do so. To formulate this alleged law in a way that is invariant with respect to the value judgments of the consumer, it would be necessary to transform it into a tautology; for example, a *rational* consumer will purchase a commodity at the best available price, where "best" means what is most worthy of rational choice. This is, clearly, not a law, but a tautological corollary of the definition of rationality. Since values are culturally variant, if generalizations about social behavior are value-laden, then it follows that such generalizations are culturally variant. Winch places heavy weight on the fact that patterns of behavior can only be understood within a framework of social traditions and rules that prescribe such behavior, so that, for example, to understand why baseball teams exchange positions in the field periodically one must cite the rules of the game, and to understand these, in turn, one must be familiar with the "form of life" of the Great American (and Japanese) Pastime.

Responses to the Challenge

Richard Rudner

Let us now consider some characteristic attempts to defend deterministic explanation in social science against this criticism. There have been many such attempts, but in examining those of Rudner and Braybrooke, two eminent philosophers of social science, I think we shall be able to see where any such defense is likely to go wrong.

In his generally excellent book *Philosophy of Social Science,* Rudner formulates, incorrectly, I believe, Winch's position and proceeds to demolish the straw man he has constructed. Rudner identifies Winch's position with that of Max Weber's method of *Verstehen,* and argues that both writers confuse two senses of "understanding":

> There are at least two senses of "understanding" at issue, one of which warrants the application of the term only if the individual to whom it applies has had certain *direct* experiences of the subject matter being "understood." "Understand" in the other sense does not have the occurrence of such experiences as a necessary condition.[4]

According to Rudner, Weber and Winch equivocate inadvertently between these two senses of "understanding" by claiming that we cannot understand meaningful social behavior without sharing the standards by which such behavior is evaluated. Rudner grants that we must share the values of the agent in order to understand the behavior in the sense of sympathetically approving of such behavior—that is, finding it meaningful in an *evaluative* sense—but we need not share values in order to understand behavior in the sense of explaining its meaningfulness in the *semantical* sense—that is, being able to state the rules, customs, and individual purposes that govern the behavior. Rudner then accuses Winch and, by implication, Weber of a fallacious equivocation between these two senses of "understanding."

> Winch's argument commits a rather subtle form of the "reproductive fallacy." . . . The claim that the only understanding appropriate to social science is one that consists of a reproduction of the conditions of states of affairs being studied, is logically the same as the claim that the only understanding appropriate to the investigation of tornadoes is that gained in the direct experience of tornadoes.[5]

There are two minor errors here, and one central error. I shall mention and then disregard the trivial ones, in order to focus on the central one.

The minor errors: Rudner conflates sharing someone's experience with sympathetically understanding it and then conflates both with evaluative understanding. Perhaps it is his own word "empathy" that detours him down the garden path. We need not directly experience a tornado in order to understand sympathetically another person's behavior in seeking shelter from the tornado. It is doubtful that either Winch or Weber ever meant to suggest such a view. In fact, Winch explicitly warns us against just such a misinterpretation, which he finds Morris Ginsberg to have perpetrated. Winch writes:

> [Weber's] characterization of *Sinn* as something "subjectively intended" must be approached warily: more warily for instance than it is approached by Morris Ginsberg, who appears to assume that Weber is saying that the sociologist's understanding of the behavior of other people must rest on an analogy with his own introspective experience.[6]

Despite this warning by Winch, Rudner identifies evaluative understanding with sympathetic understanding, and then, like Ginsberg, conflates sympathetic understanding with the empathetic reliving of an experience. Winch had attempted to forestall such misconstruals by insisting that all that *he* (and, he thinks, Weber too) means by "understanding" in social science is being able to subsume behavior under the appropriate rules. Although such understanding of others does not require us to *immerse* ourselves in others' "forms of life," that is, accept and obey their rules, it does require us to be at least *capable* of obeying such rules, in the sense of knowing how to follow them so that we can at least *imagine* ourselves doing so. Otherwise we are like a person ignorant of the rules of chess who watches a chess match but cannot hope to understand the reasons why the players make their moves.

The major error: If we set aside these erroneous reductions of evaluative understanding to sympathetic understanding, and of the latter to empathetic experiencing, we may then focus on Rudner's major claim that there are two senses of "understanding" and that Winch's argument rests on an equivocation between them. Rudner grants that understanding, in the sense of finding behavior to be evaluatively meaningful, is not the kind that causal explanation provides, but it does not follow, Rudner goes on to argue, that causal explanation cannot provide us with a more objective understanding of social phenomena. To be able to state the rules that behavior follows, and to explain why those rules were adopted, or by what historical process they came gradually into dominance, does not require that we follow those rules ourselves, or even that we be able to imagine ourselves following them. In making this claim, Rudner attempts to leap across the chasm between explanation in terms of rules and explanation in terms of causal laws. What he says about rules certainly holds of causal laws: we need not understand causal laws in an evaluative sense in order to explain their operation, but is this equally true of rules, traditions, conventions, and purposes? No doubt we can *describe or formulate* rules as well as causal laws without imagining ourselves following them. But would we, in so doing, have *explained* or come to *understand* the actions governed by those rules? If I am told that a chess player made a certain move in order to develop the queen bishop, can I possibly be said to *understand* that move if I am unable to play chess at all and thus cannot imagine myself following the same rule? On the other hand, if I am told that a planet's deviation from its expected position was due to the approach of a large asteroid, I need not imagine myself obeying the law of gravitation in order to understand the behavior of the planet. Causal laws of nature are not "obeyed" except in a metaphorical sense. The analogy between rules of human action and causal laws is a figure of speech, and the tendency to take it literally leads to serious mistakes.

Rudner, as we have seen, started out to argue against Winch's insistence that understanding human behavior is not dyadic *causal* understanding, but he went off the track by identifying normative understanding with empathetic experience, and then mistakenly argued that, since the latter is irrelevant to social science, we can go back to dyadic causal explanation with a clear conscience. But he failed to come to grips with the crucial issue as to whether normative understanding is *compatible* with causal determinism. This issue is more directly faced by Braybrooke. There are, as we shall see later, some passages in Rudner where he seems to deal tangentially with the issue. I shall fist discuss Braybrooke and then return to Rudner.

David Braybrooke

In the introduction to his anthology, *Philosophical Problems of the Social Sciences,* Braybrooke distinguishes what he calls "action questions" and "behavior questions" and argues that, while the an-swers to the first kind of questions call for purposive explanations that are non-causal, the second kind call for causal explanations, and, since both questions are always relevant, purposive or rule-governed explanations are compatible with (dyadic) causal explana-tions and social science should provide room for both. According to Braybrooke:

> The environment to be invoked in explanations of human be-havior is a social as well as a physical one. The actions of other people—cooperating or obstructing; praising or blaming; re-warding or failing to reward—provide positive and negative reinforcements that shape behavior. So long as action investi-gations take the functions of such actions into account, and so long as behavior investigations ascribe such functions to ac-tions, a continuing basis for partnership will exist.[7]

Braybrooke speaks of "behavior" explanations and then of "ev-olutionary explanations" rather than of causal explanations, but I assume that he thinks of them as causal, since he claims that they make possible prediction and control and that they employ "natural science methods." If he does not take them to be causal, then none of what I shall say applies to him, but on the other hand, it is then hard to see why he thinks there is a problem of compatibility be-tween action explanation and behavior explanation. So I shall pro-ceed on the assumption that he takes behavioral or evolutionary explanation to be one type of law-like causal explanation, while recognizing action explanation to be normative and culture-variant. This seems borne out by his example of the two types of explanation with respect to a man "handing an assortment of small gold discs to another man." Action explanation would be answers to the question:

Why is he doing it? such as: "handing them on for the next stage in engraving; or handing them back for further polishing. . . . He might be handing a month's rent to a friend; or depositing money in a bank . . . ," and so on.[8]

Behavior explanations would, according to Braybrooke, inform us "how the man . . . acquired this procedure." how "behavior in accordance with the procedure had been reinforced." and so on, presumably in accordance with the S-R laws of Skinnerian conditioning, assuming these to be causal laws.[9] Let us take a closer look at Braybrooke's example, without worrying about whether S-R laws of operant conditioning are in fact the most promising form of causal explanation of human behavior. The issue I want to focus on is whether or not such an explanation, if it *were* correct, would be compatible with the purposive explanation that A gave the coins to B in order to deposit money in the bank.

The S-R behavioral explanation, as Braybrooke conceives it, describes a causal process such that our knowledge of the antecedent causal conditions of reinforcement, the stimulus condition of A's, receiving pay and being near a bank, and the laws of conditioning enables us to predict the event of A giving the coins to B. The action explanation, to the effect that A was investing some of his money by depositing it in a savings account at 5 percent interest, informs us that A was following the rule "Save your money" and also was following the conventions of banking transactions. Thus far, neither explanation has yet adequately explained why A did what he did. What is missing from both is information as to what A hoped to accomplish by means of his action—that is, his specific purpose, such as ultimately purchasing a car or a house, or providing for his old age or for his children's education. Citation of rules and conventions is not enough for the understanding of voluntary action. We must also know what specific purpose is being served by following the rules so that we can judge whether the right rules were followed, and thus evaluate the action as wise or foolish. This fact, which Braybrooke seems to overlook, makes his partnership between the causal explanation and the action explanation collapse. For if A was following the rules of investment just because his mother had positively reinforced his thrifty behavior with lollipops and negatively reinforced his extravagances by spanking him, then his specific purpose is irrelevant to the explanation of his handing over the coins. His behavior was not rational, but compulsive, and thus not voluntary action. According to Skinner, we are always compulsive. But if so, then no action explanations are ever true, since we do what we do regardless of whether our behavior is intelligently directed toward the fulfillment of specific purposes. On such a view the rules we follow are not really rules but causal laws that we have no choice but to obey, and free action becomes rigorously predictable and controllable behavior. The action explanation—A handed the coins to B in order to deposit them in a savings account for the purpose of providing for his children's education—becomes *falsified* if the true explanation is that A handed the coins to B because he had been conditioned by his mother to put coins in his piggy bank once a week, and that the sight of the bank on this occasion was a stimulus sufficiently similar to the sight of his piggy bank to elicit the same response. If this were true, then reference to his desire to provide his children with a college education would be a false explanation.

Braybrooke systematically confuses deterministic causal explanation with historical explanation by lumping both together under the terms "behavioral" and "evolutionary."[10] Historical explanation is notoriously inconclusive. it consists in describing noteworthy events that precede the emergence of new patterns of action, and since it never shows how those antecedent events *necessitated* the pattern in questions, it never fully explains them. But this is as it should be. If the antecedent events necessitated the consequent events, the latter would not be purposive human actions and we would not be free agents. Prediction and control of individual actions, unlike prediction and control of group patterns of action, are not the proper objectives of social science, for if they were, then either it will never achieve its objectives or human beings are not free agents. In brief, the crucial issue ignored by both Rudner and Braybrooke is whether determinism is true.

Rudner Again

I mentioned earlier, *en passant,* that there is a passage in Rudner's book that appears to address itself to the problem of causal determinism, and I would like now to return to Rudner and consider his proposed solution. Rudner concedes, at least for the sake of argument, that value predicates like "right" and "good" are not definable in terms of the observable predicates required by scientific verification. Rudner then goes on to argue that this irreducibility of values to observable facts does not entail the impossibility of deterministic explanation of what Rudner calls the "observable concomitants" of value-laden action descriptions. He writes:

> The scientific validation of the types of hypothesis involved [i.e., hypotheses as to something being valued by someone] is not dependent on the *synonymy* of valuational predicates with any set of observational (or introspective) ones. All that is required for scientific validation of the relevant hypothesis is that *some* observable state of affairs be a likely concomitant of the value phenomenon in question and not that any observable state of affairs be both a necessary and sufficient condition for it.[11]

I must first hasten to observe that Rudner is not here talking directly of causal explanation, but only of confirming hypotheses as to what people value. However, I think what he says can be applied to causal explanations even more aptly than to hypotheses about values. I doubt if Winch meant to deny that we can reliably infer motives, values, customs, and rules of conduct from the observation of behavior. Winch was not critical of descriptive anthropology, but only of causal explanations of cultural phenomena. The issue is how one can confirm hypotheses as to *why* people do things like walking on hot coals or sprinkling water on newborn babies, and not as to *whether* they find value in doing so. The mere fact that they do it enthusiastically is enough to prove that they like to do it. The fact-value distinction is crucial, not to the *truth of a description* of human action, but to the *intelligibility of its explanation*. Winch would surely not deny that it is perfectly reasonable to infer that an audience enjoyed a concert from the fact that it applauded long and loud. He would only insist that the relation between hand-clapping and evaluation is culturally dependent in that audiences in some societies might express their enjoyment by foot-stamping or whistling instead, and that one has to know the appropriate rules of audience response in order to tell a bravo from a Bronx cheer. Thus a value-phenomenon can be a matter of empirical fact, but its explanation is a matter of specifying the appropriate conventions, rather than of discovering its causes. Did the audience like the concert? Yes, they clapped their hands tumultuously. Why did they clap their hands? Because that is the polite way, in our society, to express approval at a concert. Not, let us note, because hand-clapping increases social unity, or because people are operantly conditioned or genetically programmed to clap their hands at the end of a concert. If either of these explanations were correct, the applause would *not* be an index of audience approval.

But Rudner's suggestion that we consider observable concomitants of value-phenomena as the social data that are subject to scientific inquiry may be helpful in explaining why it is tempting to believe that individual and group actions are causally determined, and to believe that it is the proper goal of social science to discover their causal determinants. Much of what we do is so routine and stereotyped that it closely resembles the behavior of automata, a fact that inclines some people to believe that we *are* automata. Nowadays, a great deal of social scientific work consists of designing computer programs to simulate cognitive processes by analyzing the complex activities of human beings into strings and lattices of repetitive routines based on binary arithmetic. These simple routines are precisely the "behavioral correlates" of the activities that we describe in normative terms as skills and achievements. When a machine performs them, they can be causally explained as predictable consequences of the input data and the program. When human beings perform them, they are evaluated as right or wrong, original or trite, successful or unsuccessful. Why then can they not also be causally explained as predictable consequences of the input data (experience) and programming (cultural conditioning) of the human automaton?

I shall not attempt to answer this sixty-four thousand dollar question here. I tried to answer it in Chapter 3. Here, I merely wish to point out that this is the crucial issue that divides the Wittgensteinian position from that of defenders of deterministic social science like Rudner and Braybrooke. Thus a successful defense of causal explanation against Wittgenstein's argument would consist in reducing reason explanations to dyadic causal explanations by constructing programs that enable robots to perform individual and group actions that would be as worthy of praise and blame as are the human actions studied by the social scientist. I do not see any likelihood of such a nightmare coming true, but I cannot deny that it is logically possible. I wish only to point out that this is the real issue raised by Wittgenstein's argument, in the light of which we can understand why the argument has not yet been successfully refuted, and why it is at least not fatuous to doubt that it ever will be.

9

THE CHALLENGE OF ARTIFICIAL INTELLIGENCE

The Challenge

Functional materialism, to date the most sophisticated form of reductionism, was spawned by the computer revolution of the last three decades. And little wonder. If our computerized machines can do almost anything that human agents can do, as is now widely believed to be the case, then it would seem very likely that all our mental processes are capable of machine duplication and, if so, that mind is reducible without remainder to complex physical processes, or at least to the abstract structures (programs) instantiated by the physical processes of sufficiently complex machines. Anti-reductionists, beginning with Descartes, have been fighting a losing battle by maintaining that there are certain tasks that only human beings can perform and then, when machine programs are successfully constructed to perform those very tasks, retreating to a second, third, or nth line of defense in terms of still more sophisticated tasks such as composing original music, translating poetry, or defeating a world chessmaster. So far, computers have not been able to achieve these nth-order results. But what if, as seems likely, they eventually do? Will anti-reductionists have to surrender unconditionally to the mechanistic vision? Not, I suggest, if, and only if, they accept a distinction between dyadic, deterministic causality and triadic, indeterministic causality. Otherwise, their position has become untenable.

In *Computer Power and Human Reason,* Joseph Weizenbaum expressed grave concern over the ethical implications of the design and employment of computers to perform activities that he believes should remain the exclusive domain of human agents.[1] The glorification of machines, he maintains, results in the debasement of human beings. I share Weizenbaum's concern for the harmful effects of certain trends in computer science, but I disagree with his analysis of the cause, and with the ethical consequences he draws. I fear that in aiming at the wrong target, his sound objections to the impoverishment of our common conception of humanity will fall on deaf ears. My purpose in this chapter, therefore, is to correct Weizenbaum's aim.

After providing a lucid account of the elements of computer theory, in which he refutes some common stereotypes of what machines can and cannot "do," such as the cliché that "machines can do only what they are told to do," that is, only what can be formally derived from initial data by an algorithmic procedure, Weizenbaum concedes to militant computer theorists like A. Newell, H. Simon, and M. Minsky, that there may be nothing that humans can do that machines of the future cannot do faster and more accurately. However, Weizenbaum insists that certain activities, which he regards as the most important and ennobling of the things we do, such as creating works of art, making practical decisions that affect the lives of others, and communicating ideas and advice in conversation or in psychotherapy, *should* not be done by computers in place of human beings. Weizenbaum concludes his book with the ringing declaration:

> Computers can make judicial decisions, computers can make psychiatric judgments. . . . The point is that they ought not be given such tasks. They may even be able to arrive at "correct" decisions in some cases—but always and necessarily on bases no human being should be willing to accept. . . . What emerges as the most elementary insight is that, since we do not now have any ways of making computers wise, we ought not now to give computers tasks that demand wisdom.[2]

In many passages such as the one I have just quoted Weizenbaum concedes to the apostles of artificial intelligence, that, as Turing put it, machines can do anything that human beings can do, provided only that we can understand what we and they are doing. What is meant by the key word "understand" is that the task to be performed can be formalized, that is, adequately represented in some kind of functional notation, so that when n-1 values of the function are supplied, the nth value can be determined by computation. At times, Weizenbaum argues that the crucial fallacy lies in this definition of "understanding," because there are modes of human understanding that simply do not lend themselves to functional representation. In this contention I think Weizenbaum is profoundly right. However, insofar as he is right about this, he should have concluded that there are many things that machines cannot do, indeed, that machines can do nothing at all, in the sense of "doing" that applies to voluntary human conduct. Machines can perform computations and move through space. But doing things such as writing poetry, composing music, solving problems, learning lessons, recollecting facts, teaching students, directing and supervising the actions of others, Weizenbaum should have realized, is never reducible without remainder to the scanning and printing of symbols or to physical movements of any kind. Although physical movements are necessary components of human actions, they are never sufficient except when the action is automatic or, as we often say, "mechanical," as in the case of involuntary reflexes such as the eye blink or the knee jerk. If the problems we solve could be adequately represented in functional notation, then the solving of them would indeed be a matter of successive repetitions of physical movements corresponding to binary addition, and of course machines could do them faster and more accurately than humans. This, I think, is Weizenbaum's insight, namely, that human activities cannot be adequately formalized in functional notation. But he too often lapses from this insight into the unwise concession that machine programs can conceivably be designed to perform any human activity with great efficiency, if not with wisdom, and such a concession seems to me to defeat his case. For even if there is some property called "wisdom" that humans have and machines lack, if the same results can be achieved without this so-called wisdom, then who needs it? What I want to maintain is that Weizenbaum's concession is unnecessary; in fact, it is false.

The reason why Weizenbaum vacillates between two modalities, ought and can, with respect to what machines *ought* to do and what they *cannot* do,[3] is that he tries to arrive at ethical results without first performing linguistic surgery on the jargon of computer theorists, jargon that consists in applying psychological predicates to machine procedures and assuming that the predicates in question retain their original meanings. To go along with this game is fatal to the humanistic cause. I suggest that psychological and action predicates are improperly applied when the genuinely psychological component of their meanings is absent, namely, the component of purpose, intention, decision, or volition. As a result of his failure to note the question-begging employment of psychological language by computer theorists, Weizenbaum found it necessary to fall back on appeals to "God," "love," "authentic humanity," and vague notions of wisdom, dignity, and mysticism, notions more likely to drive us into the arms of computers than to lure us away from them.

What Can Machines Do?

My own view is that machines can do nothing; therefore, they cannot do what human beings do, in any interesting sense of the verb "to do." Solving problems is a very important kind of doing, but machines cannot solve problems. Nor, in particular, can they perform the special kind of problem-solving involved in making a rational decision. It is people who do things, with or without the aid of machines, and people who make decisions and solve problems. To solve a problem with the aid of a computer is to represent it in a machine language, transform it computationally according to programmed rules, and interpret a printout of the computational result as the solution. Without the input of data and without the interpretation of the output, there is no problem and no solution. The human input is a purposive action, and so is the interpretation of the output. All the machine itself does is mechanically or electrically transform the physical representation called the input into the physical representation called the output, that is, it transforms physical symbols into other physical symbols. The crucial element essential to thought and action that the machine cannot supply is the *interpretation* of the symbols. Take a simple computation: adding two numbers. The problem, presumably, is to answer the question: What is the sum of x plus y? You push the buttons of your calculator corresponding to the value of x and the value of y and the operation of addition, and it prints a number that represents the correct sum. Is the final printout the answer to your question? Yes, when you so interpret it; no, when it lies there uninterpreted, an inert set of marks.

The problem was to add x and y. Who solved the problem? I would think it obvious that the operator of the calculator solved it, not the calculator itself. The human operator might have solved it using an addition table, or by using her own arithmetic memory, that is, by means of the computer we call her brain. But in each such case, it is the person, not the instrument, that does the job. After all, the problem was to obtain the correct arithmetic answer; it was not just to perform a series of physical movements that correspond to binary addition. That is what the machine does, but its physical movements are not in themselves rational actions aimed at achieving a purpose desired by the machine; they are directed by the operator of the machine toward achieving the operator's purpose, which is to obtain the correct sum. If, in the course of this scenario, something were to happen that gave the operator a good reason not to bother to complete the problem-solving activity, she would desist. For example, if she saw that the room was on fire, she would disregard the calculator and run for her life. No so the machine; it would continue to work until its designated rest state was reached. Now I see no reason why this consideration does not apply equally to the most sophisticated computer procedures, such as systems of subprograms, heuristic problem-solving routines, stochastic procedures, and so on, including robotized pattern recognition, speech recognition, and any other machine processes. No matter how sophisticated the system is, it remains true that only those factors can affect the machine that it was designed and programmed to respond to. A robot might be designed and programmed to respond to a change of room temperature in a way similar to our human operator who flees a burning room, but it will so respond, not because it wants to escape injury, but because its response is determined by its design and its program. What the robot wants has nothing to do with what it does, since there is nothing it wants. But then there is nothing that it *does* (purposively). Since a robot has no problems, its behavior is incorrectly described as problem-solving, just as the pushing of the wheel of a watermill by the motion of the water is problem-solving not by the water but by the owner of the mill.

Kenneth Sayre's Defense

So far I have been making strong claims that most computer theorists (Weizenbaum is a noteworthy exception) consider plainly false. So it is time for me to offer some arguments. Space hardly permits full argumentation, but perhaps I can pinpoint the issue by refuting the argument for the opposite position as formulated persuasively by Kenneth Sayre, in his lucid book *Consciousness: A Philosophic Study of Minds and Machines*. Sayre maintains that there are no good reasons to deny, as I have just done, that computers can do things such as solving problems, while there are very good reasons to affirm that they *can* do such things. He formulates six conditions that he thinks are severally necessary and conjointly sufficient for distinguishing genuine actions from mere happenings, and he then tries to show that computers satisfy all six conditions, from which it would follow that it is a mere prejudice of species-ism, akin to racism, to deny that computers are agents.[4]

I do not consider Sayre's six conditions sufficient for agency, because he leaves out the most essential condition, namely, indeterministic causality or free will, but I shall not argue this point directly, since it will be enough to prove that computers cannot satisfy at least two of his six necessary conditions. These two conditions are:

    1. We may say that act A is properly attributable to agent x only if . . . a question of the form "why did x do A?" is appropriate . . . which cannot be answered by reference to the same events or circumstances as would adequately answer a question of the form "how did A occur" or of the form "how did x do A?" [What Sayre means here is that where agency is involved, the *why* question calls for a motive or reason, while the two *how* questions call for a narration of a sequence of physical events. I shall call this the Motive Condition.]

    2. An act is properly attributable to X as agent . . . only if it is appropriate . . . to ask . . . "Why did X do A?" but not appropriate . . . to ask . . . "Why did A happen to X?" [I shall call this the Non- Happening Condition.][5]

I intend to show that computers cannot satisfy either of these two conditions. This might seem a case of overkill, since the failure of one condition would suffice to refute Sayre, but they are so intimately interrelated that it will be instructive to consider both.

    1. Sayre's motive condition is that a motive or reason explanation be appropriate that is not also the explanation of how the event came about or how the alleged agent brought about the event. Now it seems obvious to me that computers fail this condition. "Why did the computer print out that number?" can be adequately answered by specifying its data and program, without ascribing any motives to the computer. (It may be hopelessly difficult to do this with complete specificity, but that is hardly necessary.) Sayre thinks otherwise. He

claims that the appropriate answer to the *why* question is a motivational one, namely, that "it had to do it in order to produce all the data needed for the solution of the primary problem set by the mathematician," while there is "another sort of answer appropriate to the question of *how* it solved the equation, [namely that] the program employed such-and-such heuristics."[6] Sayre's claim begs the question in assuming that machines act purposively, that they "have to" do things in order to accomplish some purpose. His claim is false, because the mere fact that the mathematician who formulated the problem wants the computer to help him solve it has no causal influence whatsoever over the computer's behavior, which is determined entirely by its design, program, and input. In brief, both the why and the how of a machine are, one would assume, physical, not psychological, and Sayre provides no good reason to believe otherwise.

2. Sayre's Non-Happening Condition is that it be semantically inappropriate to replace a genuine action description with a happening description. Thus "Why did the pavement buckle?" can be replaced by "Why did buckling happen to the pavement?" while "Why did Smith shoot Jones?" cannot be replaced by "Why did the shooting of Jones happen to Smith?" which makes no sense. Sayre then asserts that this condition "is met [by computers] since the question 'why did the computer solve the equation' is distinctly more appropriate than a question like 'why did this happen to the computer?' "[7]

Once again, Sayre begs the linguistic question. Perhaps the reason he does not notice the circularity of his argument is that it does, in fact, sound somewhat odd to say that "the solution to the equation happened to the computer." But the reason for the oddness can hardly be, as Sayre claims, that it is inappropriate to ascribe happenings to computers, if only because it is perfectly appropriate to ascribe happenings to human agents. Surely computers are not so omnipotent that nothing ever just happens to them. There are two quite different reasons for the oddness of the statement "The solution happened to the computer." One is that Sayre has stacked the deck by using the phrase "solve the equation," which is an action locution, where impartiality required that he say "the correct answer appeared on a printout," which sounds a lot more like a happening than an action. Second, we seldom speak of events happening *to* either things or agents. It sounds unnatural to say that buckling happened to the pavement, or that ignition happened to the furnace, or that slipping on a banana peel happened to the pedestrian, although none of these assertions implies voluntary agency. It is more natural to say that the pavement buckled, the furnace ignited, the pedestrian slipped. That this is a trivial fact of English style and not evidence of agency is clear when we consider that we may employ infinitives to make happening descriptions quite natural, as when we say: The pavement happened to buckle, or the furnace happened to ignite, or the man happened to slip. But where genuine agency is involved, we cannot similarly replace the action description with a happened-to clause. For example, we cannot say "Smith happened to shoot Jones" without giving the false impression that Smith behaved in an accidental or unintentional way, such as aiming at what he thought was a bear and *happening to* hit Jones instead.

The reason for Sayre's mistake is instructive. The argument depends on superficial features of linguistic usage, rather than on an adequate analysis of the difference between action and happening. The essential difference is that happenings are brought about by antecedent causes alone, while actions are not, for if they were, they would not be attributable to an agent. When we can prove that what occurred, such as the buckling of the pavement, or slipping on a banana peel, was a necessary result of antecedent events such as high temperature or the convergence of foot with banana peel, we have established that voluntary agency was not involved, that motives and reasons are irrelevant, and the "happened-to" locution becomes appropriate. Now where computer processes are at work, we can always explain the result as a necessary consequence of the antecedent causes, that is, the design, program, and input. Consequently, machine processes are happenings, not actions.

Members of the "artificial intelligentsia" will be quick to retort that this discussion is making a big deal of something quite trivial, the fact that psychological language is misused when applied to machines. It might be conceded that when we speak of machines solving problems and making decisions we should put these expressions in quotation marks so as to acknowledge that they are being employed in a special, jargonistic way. But how serious an error can it be if we just don't bother with quotation marks?

Intelligence and Routine Performance

Of course, the issue is not the words, with or without quotation marks. The issue is what we understand by our use. The fundamental issue is a metaphysical one: whether the rational decisions of human agents are fully explainable by neurological processes that can be duplicated by machines. I discussed this issue at length in an earlier book, *Persons*.[8] Here I shall confine myself to pointing out that, if this deterministic hypothesis is true, then our concept of a person as a conscious and free agent, endowed with the cognitive authority to define his or her own values, purposes, and interests and with responsibility for one's actions, is an illusory luxury destined to go the way, as Richard Rorty and P. K. Feyerabend have suggested, of the ancient belief in witchcraft and demoniacal possession.[9] The adoption of such a standpoint has enormous eth-ical consequences, for it leads us to believe that a human agent has no more claim on our respect for his or her autonomy than a machine, since he or she is as subject to causal manipulation, such as repro-gramming, as any other machine. This is precisely the conclusion drawn by B. F. Skinner in his book, *Beyond Freedom and Dignity*. It also leads people to believe that whatever human beings do that cannot be defined in functional notation is too vague and irrational to be worth doing. Thus Marvin Minsky writes:

> There are already programs that write music which, although bad, is better than most people can write. To write really good music or draw highly meaningful pictures will of course require better semantic models in these areas. That these are not avail-able is not so much a reflection on the state of heuristic programs as on the traditionally disgraceful state of analytic criticism in the arts—a cultural consequence of the fact that most esthetic analysts wax indignant when it is suggested that it might be possible to understand what they are trying to understand.[10]

Minsky seems to be saying that, whatever aspects of human ac-tivity, in particular, the creative aspects, cannot be formalized in a machine program cannot be understood. What is unformalizable is unintelligible. Weizenbaum aptly compares this attitude to the drunkard who looks for his lost keys across the street from where he dropped them because, as he explains to a policeman, "the light is better over here."

The reason why we employ machines to get our work done is the same as the reason we train ourselves to act in mechanically routine ways, up to a certain point. In learning to typewrite, to swim, to dance, to drive a car, or to perform any skillful and complex activity, we deliberately condition our bodies to respond to a limited number of stimuli in an automatic way, such as stepping on the brake at the sight of a red light, so that we can focus our attention on less routine factors that require creative variation. Apostles of artificial intelligence tend to identify intelligence with the routine, automatic responses that require intelligence on our part to learn to perform *initially*, but are precisely the aspects of our activities that we train our bodies to perform *without* intelligent attentiveness, just in order to free our attention for the unpredictable factors that call for creative responses. No doubt machines can grind out mathematical results and trite musical harmonies more effectively than most people. But that is only to say that they can be used to perform the routine subtasks that we otherwise must train the parts of our own bodies, including our brains, to perform automatically. Tasks that require considerable intelligence on the part of an untrained person can be done mechanically and unthinkingly by a highly trained person, and therefore also and more efficiently by the use of a machine. But it does not follow, either that the machine is doing them, or that an expert, in doing them routinely, is exercising intelligence. Only *learning* to do them is an exercise of intelligence. And despite what some computer apostles claim, computers do not learn; they carry out inductive strategies, not because they want to solve a problem, since they do not have wants, but because they are programmed to employ them. It would be absurd to say that a creature has learned to do what it does not at all want to do (although behavioral psychologists do say it)—for example, that in acquiring bad habits like smoking we learn to ruin our health, or that a badly taught student learns how to fail exams. Learning implies progress toward a desired goal. Consequently, what is done without purpose is misdescribed as learning, no matter how sophisticated the inductive principles may be that govern the process.

The general point I want to make is that psychological concepts, such as learning, deciding, and intending are improperly applied to machines unless their use is avowedly metaphorical. Many philosophers who should know better make this mistake. For example, J. C. Smart, in *Philosophy and Scientific Realism,* maintains that when psychological concepts are clearly defined, either behaviorally or structurally (in terms of internal processes that explain behavior), there remains no reason why machines cannot be designed to manifest those defining features. Indeed, he claims, machines can already be said to pursue purposes or goals, and there is no theoretical obstacle to designing machines that would be conscious, have feelings and thoughts, exhibit values in preferential behavior, and even enter into social relationships such as friendships and love affairs.[11]

Norman Malcolm effectively debunked these flights of fantasy in *Memory and Mind.* Malcolm pointed out that the belief that machines can simulate the mental processes of human beings starts from the false semantic premise that psychological concepts designate definite *processes,* either mental processes or neurological processes, that go on inside the human skull. If this premise were correct, then of course we need only identify such processes clearly in order to devise isomorphic machine processes to duplicate them. To reveal the absurdity of this premise, Malcolm invites us to consider four situations in which we would say that a man wants to catch a bus:

Case 1. The man is eating breakfast, sees his bus approaching, jumps up and grabs his coat, and runs full speed toward the bus stop.

Case 2. He sees the bus passing his house, imagines his boss firing him, and groans in despair.

Case 3. He hears the bus approaching and says to his wife: "God, do I want to catch that bus!"

Case 4. He is shaving, looks out the window and sees the bus passing by, shrugs his shoulders, and continues shaving since there is nothing he can do about the bus.[12]

Malcolm challenges us to try to imagine any internal process involved in each of these four cases that could serve as the designatum of the expression "wants to catch the bus." Notice that the four cases involve four quite different criteria for judging that the man wants to catch the bus. In the first case the criterion is behavioral—his running toward the bus stop. In the second, it is his image of being fired and his emotions of sorrow and fear. In the third, it is his declaration to his wife, and in the fourth, it is simply the historical fact that he always takes that bus at that time. In this last case it is obvious that there is nothing going on inside him that could be considered the *process* of wanting to catch the bus. Consequently, there is no way to reproduce or even simulate in a machine the various kinds of conditions for the correct application of a psychological predicate like "want to catch the bus," since there is no unitary process that is a common factor in all these conditions.

I turn now to the ethical consequences of the view that I share with Weizenbaum, despite the differences just indicated. Machines are instruments of human will, like our arms and legs and brains. By means of them we achieve purposes that it would be difficult or impossible to achieve without them. I cannot therefore see anything wrong with employing machines to perform any task that we have a right to perform without their aid. Weizenbaum argues that we should not allow machines to make judicial decisions, or to interpret and simulate human speech by recording and issuing vocal commands, or to respond to patients in psychoanalytic sessions, or to wage war. With respect to making judicial decisions, I have already argued that machines cannot make *any* decisions. They can of course match input descriptions of offenses against prescribed penalties and print out the appropriate penalties, and they are now so functioning in many traffic courts. But the reasonable objection to this procedure is not that machines should not be doing the work of bored and thoughtless judges, but that our judges should not be so bored and thoughtless that machines can do their work better than they. No one should respond in so automatic a manner as to remove adjudication from the area of thoughtful decision, whether by using machines or by not using one's own head. I feel far less resentment toward the computer that prints out my fine for a traffic offense than toward a human judge who regards me as a datum to be processed, because I know that the machine is incapable of responding to the unique aspects of my case while the human judge is not incapable, but uninterested.

Again, although research in speech recognition and simulated response may well be a waste of money that could be better used elsewhere, I cannot agree with Weizenbaum that there is anything sinister in programming machines to record and simulate speech. I agree that innocuous private telephone conversations should not be spied upon, but human eavesdropping is just as objectionable as machine recording. I do not fancy being answered by a computer when I telephone an office, but no more do I fancy the automatic responses I get from officious receptionists.

As for psychotherapy by computers, the mere fact that Colby's DOCTOR program for non-directive therapy was found by many psychotherapists to do a good job only confirms my long-held suspicion that psychotherapy is a rip-off no matter who or what performs it. Weizenbaum claims that proper psychotherapy requires a loving relationship between therapist and patient. That claim would be disputed by the therapist who was recently sued for malpractice by a patient with whom he had a love affair. As for waging war, it seems to me just as evil if less efficient to strangle people with one's bare hands as to employ computerized missile systems to kill them. In general, it is just as wrong and no more wrong to do by means of machines anything that it is wrong to do without them. To rely on machines to make our decisions for us is therefore not immoral, as Weizenbaum suggests, but it is plainly foolish, because machines cannot make decisions. They can only perform automatic responses in situations that have been *removed* from the area of decision. I have argued that our own human tendency to respond habitually, un-thinkingly, and routinely to many situations that call for thoughtful and creative response is a deplorable phenomenon, of which the ex-cessive reliance on computers is only a special case. The fundamental problem is man's inhumanity to man. To paraphrase Shakespeare, the fault is not in our computers, but in ourselves.

10

KEEPING MIND
AND BODY TOGETHER

Two Issues: Mind and Interaction

This, the final chapter, offers the patient reader a bonus. It has been argued that distinguishing two kinds of causality, one deterministic, the other indeterministic, enables us to make coherent sense of our assignments, transfers, and reductions of moral responsibility, to clear up some conceptual confusions that plague therapeutic psychology and the social sciences, and to understand why machine simulations of human performances are simulations only, not replications. The proposed distinction will, I think, do even more for us; it will provide a dramatic payoff of special interest to philosophers of mind: a low-cost solution to the perennial mind-body problem. The solution will require two stages: (1) the explanation of what mind is and how it differs from body, and (2) the explanation of how mind causally interacts with body.

The mind-body problem, simply stated is: How can two things so utterly different as mind and body affect each other; how can the body illuminate or cloud the mind, causing it to register pain, pleasure, sensation, and ideas, and how can the mind direct and innervate the body, causing it to carry out the mind's intentions, plans, and purposes? What is the causal process that carries influence from one to the other; is it a mental process or a bodily process? If the first, how can it do any physical work; if the second, how can it do any mental work?

This family of questions is atrociously loaded. Who says the mind and body are so utterly different that neither a bodily nor a mental process could connect them? Descartes said so and then shrank from the logical consequences, desperately searching for some kind of neutral process, quasi-physical and quasi-mental, to rebuild the bridge he had made impossible. In Cartesian terms, as Spinoza, Leibniz, and Malebranche noted, the mind-body problem is as insoluble as squaring the circle.

But then why are we so bemused by it? Even W. I. Matson and John Searle, who claim that Aristotle solved it long before Descartes raised it, seem to imply that there is, or at least was, a mind-body problem, even if they consider it less vexing than writers in the Cartesian tradition. But if the above Cartesian formulation of the problem is unacceptably question-begging, then what is the alternative formulation in terms of which it becomes tractable enough to have been solved by Aristotle, or by anyone else? Matson's formulation of the solution is: the mind is the activity of the body;[1] Searle's is: the mind is to the body as digestion is to the stomach.[2] Good, but what was the problem to which these formulations offer the solution? Is anyone perplexed by the problem of how digestion can affect or be affected by the stomach? We seem to be offered a solution to which no problem corresponds. At least, no philosophical problem. One might wonder what physical changes in the stomach produce various types of good or bad digestion and how, in turn, the digestive processes nourish or injure the stomach tissue, but these straightforward factual questions are for the physiologist to answer, and they are certainly not answered by asserting the tautology that digestion is the normal activity of the stomach. But it is claimed that asserting that mind is the functional activity of the body really solves the mind-body problem. So if the claim is sound, then the mind-body problem cannot be the kind of family of factual inquiries that physiologists handle, and for which the Aristotelian definition of mind as the form or activity of the body provides no further illumination.

Let's put our cards on the table. Everyone who thinks about it, Cartesian or anti-Cartesian, feels perplexity about mind-body inter-action. But perhaps the Aristotelian solution recommended by Matson and Searle was meant as an answer to our first question: what is mind? rather than the second: how do mind and body affect each other? And perhaps the appeal, for them, of this as an answer to the first question is that it renders the second question unintelligible and therefore not in need of any answer. If the mind is the effective functional activity of the body, rather than a substance different from it but somehow residing in it, then no question of interaction can or need arise. No one is perplexed by how a knife can affect or be affected by its cutting, nor how a bus can interact causally with its passengers' transportation. Perhaps then what Matson and Searle are telling us is that there seems to be a problem only when we think of the mind, as Descartes did, as a distinct substance, rather than as a mode of bodily functioning. If so, think they are substantially right (forgive the pun), yet I am still nagged by a fly-in-the-bottle perplexity about mind-body interaction and, furthermore, by a meta-perplexity about why I feel there is a vexing problem even when I refrain from picturing the mind as a ghostly ectoplasm inside the skull. Any dissolution of the problem by some form of materialism must, I think, explain why there is so powerful an appearance of a problem, before dispelling the appearance, or else one is left wondering what there was to dispel. It is not much of a magician's trick to make a rabbit disappear from a hat if we do not first see a rabbit in the hat, even if it is an illusory rabbit.

Matson, Searle, et al. are right that thinking of the mind and the body as distinct things having no shareable or transferable properties makes the problem of interaction insoluble. But suppose we avoid this Cartesian cul-de-sac by talking only about mental and physiological events, that is, changes of mental and bodily states, rather than about the mind and the body. We still want to know how one of these types of events or processes (understanding processes as causal sequences of events) can bring about the other, that is, what processes mediate between them, providing a causal bridge from the mental to the physical and vice versa. This is not, at least not obviously, a question loaded with Cartesian metaphysics. But even in this more neutral form, the functionalist account of mind does not seem to allow it to be intelligible, let alone provide an illuminating answer to it.

What functionalism (in its deterministic form in Matson, Searle, Ryle, Dennett, et al.) and dualism have in common is a still deeper assumption that I have been disputing throughout this study, namely, that mental and physiological processes, whatever they may be, can produce each other directly, without the mediation of the human agent, who, I have been arguing, is the indispensable middleman, the bridge between mind and body that Descartes searched for in vain. The assumption of direct connection is what I have been at pains to refute. With this in mind, let's go back to the first question: What is mind?

What Is Mind?

We have seen enough reason to assume that the mind is not an immaterial substance having no properties in common with matter.

We need a definition of mind that will do justice to its distinctive features, such as intentionality, first-person authority or privacy, and creative intelligence, and yet will render the problem of interaction with bodily states capable of solution without having to deny the very appearance of the problem.

Reductive materialists claim that mental states are a subset of bodily states, governed by the same fundamental laws of physics and chemistry and the same causal processes. The most persuasive reason for accepting this claim is that it makes the problem of causal interaction deliciously tractable. Of course, one type of bodily state can interact with another type of bodily state. No problem. This solution, unlike the Aristotelian functionalism of Matson and Searle, is at least illuminating, if true, since it is conceptually possible for one type of physical state to interact causally with another type, whereas it is not possible for the functional activity of an entity to interact causally with the entity whose activity it is. Furthermore, on the reductionist account, the problem is straightforwardly conceptual, whereas on the functionalist account, it is replaced by a family of empirical inquiries as to which changes in structure produce which changes of function and vice versa, inquiries that engender no philosophical perplexity whatsoever.

How well does reductionism solve the mind-body problem? Too well, I suggest. If the mind is identical with a part or aspect of the body, such as the cerebral processes, then of course interaction is possible; there is no reason for perplexity. Why then were we perplexed? Are we genetically programmed or indoctrinated in the cradle to be Cartesian dualists? Or does our perplexity not really disappear, but become transferred to another question that then becomes as baffling as was that of interaction, namely, how can any part or aspect of the body have the distinctively mental features of intentionality, privacy, and creative adaptability? Since property dualism is not much of an advance over substantial dualism, the reductionist is compelled to deny that mental properties are as distinctive as we took them to be, and to claim that their distinctiveness is an illusion stemming from our ignorance of their complex physical composition. But if they are right, then neither mind nor its distinctive features exist, after all, and psychology is a theoretically superfluous surrogate for as yet unavailable physico-chemical knowledge. The mind-body problem has been solved with a vengeance, by reducing it to a mindless body problem. That is an exorbitant price to pay for liberation from philosophical perplexity. I think I can propose a better deal.

Ever since the appearance, in 1959, of J. J. C. Smart's program for reducing mental states to brain states,[3] materialists have been engaged in the project of redefining mind-body identity in order to soften the reductive impact of making psychology theoretically superfluous. The first step was to replace Smart's strict identity with a weaker relation called "theoretical identity" by its proponents, Jerome Shaffer, Joseph Cornman, Thomas Nagel, et al.,[4] and the second step was to introduce a still weaker relation of functional equivalence, espoused by Hilary Putnam, Jerry Fodor, and Daniel Dennett.[5] Finally, Donald Davidson suggested a retreat from any kind of type relation to identity of particular events, a sense of identity that is so weak as to approach empirical vacuity.[6] For in this sense, any mental event can be claimed without fear of refutation to be identical with any concurrent and proximate bodily event, for example, my annoyance with the late arrival of the newspaper this morning with the flexing of my left toe at the same moment. Since neither event will ever be repeated, no predictions that could serve as confirmation or disconfirmation follow from the identity claim.

Together with the weakening of the identity hypothesis, the above writers have also restored autonomy to psychological explanation of

human conduct, thereby resisting explanatory reduction as a corre-
late of ontological reduction and so preserving, it might seem, the
indispensability of psychology and the social sciences. At least, that
is what they were trying to do. Whether they succeeded is what I
want to question. Their common mistake, which I think doomed
their enterprise from the outset, was to hold fast to causal determinism, the one belief that should have been abandoned if their project
was to have any chance of success.

The most moderate of these materialists, proposing the least painful break with common sense beliefs, were Davidson and Dennett,
who conceded that our knowledge of mind is imprecise, unreliable,
and bereft of genuine causal laws and that the explanations we give
of mental states and intentional actions are quite different from, and
not mere approximations to, covering-law explanations of natural
science. Yet despite this crucial concession they continued to hold, in
common with reductive materialists like Smart, that psychological
and sociological explanations are causal in just the same sense of
"causal" as their big brothers, while granting that they are not now
and probably never will be grown up enough to achieve the same
degree of precision and reliability. Davidson is more cautious than
Dennett on this score, since Dennett holds that psychological explanations in terms of intentions, beliefs, and desires are indispensable
only pragmatically, insofar as we do not yet and perhaps never will
know, or in any case will always find it unbearably inconvenient to
find out, purely physical explanations of voluntary actions, but that
it is in principle possible to do so and thus to dispense with "folk
psychology." Davidson remains more faithful to common sense opinion in considering it a necessary truth that mental predicates are not
reducible to physical predicates and that the workings of the mind
are therefore not adequately explicable in terms of the concepts and
laws of the natural sciences.

Most materialists, and even crypto-dualists like A. C. Danto (who calls himself a "retentive materialist,"[7] but whose *Analytical Philosophy of Action* seems to me clearly dualistic), assume that we have plenty of laws of psychology and sociology, as well as psychophysical and physico-psychological laws, so that psychological explanations, if fully fleshed out, would have the same structure and mesh smoothly with explanations in the natural sciences, even granted that the former are vaguer, less predictably potent, and more trite than the latter. Davidson is almost alone in holding that the vagueness, predictive impotence, and triteness of psychological generalizations are symptoms of a deep difference that disqualifies them from being early approximations of the laws of nature.

Moderates tend, when pushed hard, to become polarized and fall back into the camp of those whose extremism they have been trying to moderate. I think we will find this as true in philosophy as it is in politics. When probed and pressed, Davidson's view will collapse into Dennett's, and Dennett's into the radical reductionism of Smart, Lewis, Feyerabend, Rorty, and Churchland.[8]

The crucial issue is *causal laws*. Are mind and purposive action governed by causal laws or not? Most materialists beg this question in the affirmative by simply assuming that there are such laws and that we are already in possession of enough of them to make it likely that the others await our discovery. Smart, Fodor, Danto, Putnam, Churchland, and Lewis all speak casually of "the laws" of psychology and sociology.[9] Davidson and Dennett are more cautious. They believe that there are law-like relations at work, but they recognize that we do not now and perhaps never will have them within epistemological reach, because the trite but indispensable generalizations of "folk" psychology are not even approximations to law-like causal relations. Dennett seems to hold that the fact that we cannot yet and perhaps never will be able to formulate genuine psycho-physical laws doesn't matter, because psychological explanations are in principle, although not in fact, replaceable by physiological explanations. Davidson thinks it does matter, because the former do a different job and are irreplaceable even in principle. Let us explore this difference of opinion to see just how deep it goes.

Dennett distinguishes three kinds of explanation: intentional, design, and physical.[10] He holds that computer science has achieved a breakthrough in mind-body metaphysics by producing computers whose behavior can, *pragmatically speaking,* be explained only by the computational strategies of rational agents, that is, by the problem to be solved and the best method for solving it. This is the way we explain the actions of persons. But he also maintains that such intentional explanations are, in principle, replaceable by descriptions of the physical hardware and functional software of the computer, that is, by design explanations. This is not practically feasible because such design explanations would be unbearably complex. The situation is similar to explaining and predicting weather changes. We know most of the laws that govern such changes, but the initial conditions are so complex that it would take too much time and effort to measure them precisely enough to derive exact predictions of high reliability. So in practice we settle for rough approximations guided by qualitative generalizations based upon past experience rather than deduced from initial conditions and laws. But no one doubts that the progress of meteorology will bring it ever closer to the ideal of exact prediction. Similarly, according to Dennett, intentional explanations serve as useful stopgaps that are in principle replaceable by design explanations that, in turn, are theoretically replaceable by purely physical explanations in terms of fundamental particles and energy transactions. In this way Dennett seems to preserve the best of both worlds: (*a*) the practical indispensability of common sense psychology and ethics, and (*b*) causal determinism and the unity of science. Nevertheless, if intentional explanation is merely a convenient stopgap and not the deep and true type of explanation as Dennett holds, in common with eliminative materilists like Churchland, Rorty, and Feyerabend, then it is only the empirical unavailability of design and physical explanations that protects psychology and ethics from what the British whimsically call "redundancy," that is, unemployment.

The indispensability of psychological explanation is, for Dennett, illusory, for it is guaranteed not by our knowledge but by our ignorance, somewhat like the magical powers of the prestidigitator in the eyes of the naive spectator. In brief, Dennett's view differs from the radical materialism of Smart & Co. only on the issue of pragmatic feasibility, but not on the bottom (i.e., metaphysical) line, that mental events and states are complex relations of physical events and states.

Davidson's view is more subtle. For him, mental states and their explanatory roles are neither law-like in themselves, nor even in principle replaceable by bodily states and their explanatory roles. Nonetheless they are, he maintains, identical to particular bodily states that *are* deterministically predictable from initial conditions and laws of neurophysiology, although we cannot know *which* bodily states they are identical with. He rightly points out that from the identity of a mental state with a bodily state it does not follow that whatever explains the latter also explains the former, because an explanation must be in the right linguistic form to do its job and physical explanations are, for several reasons that Davidson delineates at length, inappropriate to the explanation of mental states and intentional actions.[11] These reasons are the following:

1. Intentional states and actions require to be explained in terms that are logically related to them, so that the cause cited must be described in intentional or purposive language. For example, Susan

went to the movies because she wanted to forget her troubles and believed that would be the best way to accomplish the purpose. On the assumption that Susan was acting rationally (which we must make in order to provide an intentional explanation—see reason 3 below) the explicans entails the explicandum.[12] The tautological character of the explanation accounts for the triteness of psychological generalizations as compared with causal laws in the natural sciences.[13]

2. Psychological explanations are holistic: to understand an intentional action fully we must see it as part of a pattern involving all or at least many of the beliefs, desires, and values of the agent, which is why, according to Davidson, it would be a hopeless task to look for precise and non-trivial laws of psychology.

3. There is an "irreducibly normative element in all attributions of attitude,"[14] which cannot be formulated in non-normative physical terms. Dennett agrees with this claim and explains it nicely as due to the assumption of rationality necessary to get intentional explanation off the ground.[15] We cannot explain the behavior of creatures whose values and purposes are totally different from our own; indeed it seems doubtful that we could even recognize that they have *any* values and purposes. On the other hand, if we were to insist that normative considerations enter into the formulation of laws of nature, we would turn the clock back to the era of entelechies and final causes. Davidson's reasons, while sound enough, are not compelling, since it may be argued that, to some extent at least, they are also true of explanations in natural science, in the following ways:

1. Davidson himself has argued that tautological explanations, such that the explicans entails or is entailed by the explicandum, are not necessarily invalidated as satisfactory causal explanations even in natural science, for example, "He has a burn because he was burned" and "The lunar eclipse was caused by the interposition of

the earth between the sun and the moon" (Aristotle). Yet he cites the logical connections between explicans and explicandum as a reason why psychological generalizations are not law-like. Perhaps there is no real inconsistency here. Perhaps he means that, in psychological explanation, *any* adequate description of the cause will entail or be entailed by any adequate description of the effect, whereas in natural science, tautologically worded explanations such as the two above can always be restated in terms that satisfy Hume's condition of logical independence. Even so, the fact that non-psychological explanations *can* be tautological in form somewhat weakens the impact of the logical connections argument for an unbridgeable gap between psychology and natural science.

2. To some extent all explanations, to be precise and complete, would have to take account of minor influences exerted by the entire cosmos, for example, the slight gravitational forces from distant galaxies. Thus, to be completely adequate, all explanations should be holistic. Of course, we never demand perfect precision, completeness, or adequacy. In scientific explanations we cut off minor influences and settle for a specifiable margin of inaccuracy. But why then not do so in psychology as well and thus escape the requirement of holistic explanation? No doubt the degree of holistic interdependence of facts in psychology is far greater than in natural science so that the acceptable margin of error has to be considerably greater, and thus Davidson is right on the issue of degree. But matters of degree lack the compelling force of sharp distinctions of kind, so that this consideration, like the previous one, may fail to persuade us to deny law-like status to psychological generalizations.

3. The inexpungeably normative element in psychological explanations appealed to be Davidson would seem to be due to this: in order to understand why an agent performs an action, or even to identify the action performed, we must assume that the agent is

rational in the sense that he or she employs the best means (given the agent's beliefs and desires) to achieve the goal, and "best" is of course evaluative. However, it is often pointed out that there are normative aspects of explanation in the applied natural sciences such as engineering, meteorology, or medicine. The explanation of why a bridge collapsed, or a tumor formed in someone's liver, employs normative standards such as adequate strength of materials, normal versus abnormal metabolism, and so on. Davidson is entitled to insist that psychology involves a greater degree of relativity to normative standards (perhaps I should say, relativity to a greater degree of variability of standards) than applied natural science, but again, a difference of degree hardly carries the argumentative force of a difference of kind.

But these three inconclusive reasons of Davidson's are symptoms of a deeper distinction that does justify a sharp division between mental and physical explanation, even within the limits of Davidson's analysis of mental states and intentional action. The crucial difference, which underlies these, but which he does not acknowledge, lies in the directed purposive character of mental states and intentional actions, which cannot be captured by physical events and processes. How then can Davidson consistently hold that mental events are, even in his very weak sense, identical to physical events? I cannot demonstrate an inconsistency in this regard, although I feel it in my bones. But I think I can demonstrate a related possible inconsistency, the avoidance of which would undermind Davidson's identity claim, or else force his position back to Dennett's that, in principle, psychology is replaceable by neurophysiology.

Assume, following Davidson, that a mental state M that causes an action A is identical to a particular brain state B, and that action A is identical to a particular bodily movement E of the agent, which produced some desired change in the environment. The agent's brain state B is caused by a physical stimulus S, together with the structural features F of the agent's brain (its hardware plus its program), and this causal relation, since it is physical, is, for Davidson, law governed; that is, there is a law that, under standard conditions, every instance of the type of physical event to which S belongs, in conjunction with an instance of the type of neurological structure to which F belongs, will be followed by an instance of the type of brain state to which B belongs. But, says Davidson, there is no physicopsychological bridge law that all instances of the type of which S belongs will be followed by a mental state of the type to which M belongs. Nonetheless, according to Davidson, M is identical to B and A to E. Now, as Cornman has pointed out,[16] once the identity of reference of two terms is established, it follows that whatever is true of one is true of the other, so that if B is derivable by laws from S, then so also is M, in principle, if not in feasible fact. But then there must be physio-psychological bridge laws, if Davidson's identity claim is true, although such laws would be rather odd: they would have the peculiar feature of applying only to single instances, such as the one M that is identical to the instance B that follows from S and F and L. Thus to avoid this inconsistency, Davidson must either retract his identity claim or else relinquish the irreplaceability of psychology with neurophysiology.

The same difficulty arises with respect to the explanation of intentional actions. If, as Davidson holds, an action A is identical to a bodily movement E and, as above, the agent's mental state M that causes A is identical to a brain state B produced by stimulus S, then, since B is derivable from S in conjunction with physical laws L, and E is derivable from B together with other laws (of neurophysiology) L', it follows that E is derivable from the conjunction of B with L and L', and so, given A = B, is A, even if, *pace* Davidson, A is not adequately explainable in this way. Derivability is transitive across

identity, even if explainability is not. Thus if we knew the physiological laws that govern the effects of physical stimuli on the nervous
system and the laws that govern muscular responses to those effects,
then, as Dennett holds, we could reduce intentional actions to physiological responses and dispense with psychological language, so that
the only reason we need psychology is that we lack adequate knowledge of the relevant laws, L and L'. But then psychology, with or
without the bridge laws that Davidson insists are unavailable, is
pragmatically indispensable only because of our ignorance, and is
therefore theoretically redundant. Davidson's view has collapsed into
Dennett's, which, we already found, collapses into the reductivism of
Smart & Co.

Davidson's problems stem from his assumption that "cause" has
the same meaning in psychology as in physics and is equally deterministic in both employments. He rightly insists that an agent's
beliefs and desires cannot be known to necessitate her actions, nor
can her receptions of physical stimuli be known to necessitate her
beliefs and desires, because the relations involved are not law-like.
Yet he clings to the belief that psychological causality is, underneath
it all, deterministic and there are, in fact, causal laws governing the
relations between physical and mental states, maintaining only that,
because of the peculiar features of psychological explanation that we
have already discussed, we can never discover those laws. Thus, on
his view, while psychological explanations will always *appear* law-
lessly indeterministic, the mental processes that go on inside us are
in fact deterministic, but in ways too subtle to be known because the
mental-physical identities involved are unknowable. In order to save
psychological determinism, Davidson pays the exorbitant price of
postulating an unverifiable identity between particular mental states
and particular bodily states, so as to transfer law-governed determinism from body to mind, while at the same time preserving the

autonomy of psychology by denying that the explanations provided by physical laws and initial conditions can be transferred. With such mirrors are maidens bloodlessly sawed in two.[17]

I propose now to go directly to the heart of the trouble with any deterministic view of the mind, whether dualist, or reductive materialist, or functionalist. Hilary Putnam astutely observed that the essence of mechanism is not materialism, but determinism.[18] Assuming determinism, the functionalist account of mind as a computer program is as compatible with dualism as with materialism. On the other hand, if the mind is not a computer program, that is not due to its being an incorporeal substance (so is a program, after all), but to its not operating in an algorithmic way that would enable us to formulate laws by means of which its outputs could be deduced from its inputs.

The difference between materialism and dualism, as Putnam noted, is irrelevant to the mind-body problem. Whatever kind of entity mind may be, whether corporeal or spiritual, the essential feature that distinguishes it from matter is, as Davidson sensed but could not quite countenance, that its workings are subject to moral evaluation because of its freedom from causal determinism—in a work, its lawlessness.

Returning to the question with which we began, how does this discussion help to solve the mind-body problem? I believe it helps in the following way:

How Is Interaction Possible?

Everyone knows that Cartesian dualism engendered an insoluble mind-body problem, but not everyone seems to know that reductive materialism makes that problem disappear by making the mind disappear with it. The truth, I think, must lie somewhere in between. An adequate conception of mind should offer a safe channel between the Scylla of substantial dualism and the Charybidis of reductive materialism, by doing justice to the irreducibility of mental states while also avoiding any picture of the mind as a ghostly substance that mysteriously interacts with the body in violation of the principle of conservation of energy. I want to propose such a safe channel in the form of a functional account of mind that differs from the mechanistic functionalism of Davidson, Dennett, Lewis, Putnam, Searle, et al. in two respects: (1) My view, unlike theirs, distinguishes psychological causality from physical causality, recognizing the former to be traidic and indeterministic, and (2) on my view a person is not identical with a mind nor with a body, but is the owner of both, the indispensable middle link between thought and action.

My indeterministic functional view of mind is as follows: A mental process is neither a physical process nor a non-physical process. It is the minimally intelligent *use* an organism makes of its body and the capacity for such use, and it involves both physiological and purposive features. When our sense organs are stimulated, we think, feel, and act. Thinking, feeling, and acting are mental processes that involve physiological changes and interactions between our bodies and their environment, although sometimes, when we merely think or daydream, those interactions are minimal. What makes these processes mental is that they are minimally intelligent uses of our bodies to achieve our purposes, uses that cannot be uniquely determined by antecedent conditions because they depend on our *ad hoc* assessments and revisions of our priorities.

When we perceive objects and form beliefs about them, it seems as if we are passive recipients of sensory stimulation and it doesn't seem as if we *do* anything. How then can it be maintained that such passive mental processes are uses of our bodies? I think the difference here between activity and passivity is a matter of degree of likelihood of alternative responses and that, because this is a matter of degree, we are seldom, if ever, absolutely passive even in perceiving things and forming beliefs about them. When the perceptual field is ambiguous, for example, a mass of unfamiliar faces among whom a friend or an enemy may be present, the observer forms tentative beliefs: this face appears benign, that one looks sinister. There is room for some choice as to what one perceives attentively, subsequent to the formation of such tentative hypotheses, if only a choice about what to bring into focus, like a newspaper or television cameraman at a sports event or a political demonstration. Normally, however, perceiving seems to go on all by itself, without selective effort. Light strikes our eyes and we see an object. Sound strikes our eardrums and we hear thunder or cannon fire. How can such automatic seeing and hearing be uses of our bodies? Use would seem to imply active choice of means to ends.

But consider what happens when one performs an automatic action such as brushing one's teeth. The movements of the limbs seem to occur without thought or decision. One is seldom aware of hesitation between alternative possible movements of hands and fingers. Yet surely one is doing something, and using one's body to get it done. Choice among alternatives is not normally involved unless there is some ambiguity in the situation, say, two brushes of the same color, or an arthritic twitch in one's favored arm. Yet can we not be said to be acting voluntarily, even when there is no hesitation because there are no significant alternatives to choose among? I don't see why not, except that we simply don't bother to distinguish voluntary from involuntary *automatic* behavior, provided that the indulgence of a habit is not so harmful as to suggest compulsion. As Ryle and Austin noted, we only bother to distinguish voluntary from involuntary behavior in situations that raise questions of responsibility. And such situations do, of necessity, present significant alternatives. Even so, it is fair to ask: What type of conduct does our toothbrushing example resemble more closely—standard voluntary action or standard reflex responses such as sneezing? It seems obvious to me that normal habitual behavior is closer to the former type since it fulfills the agent's purpose; it is something she does intentionally. Now I want to suggest that the same is true of perception and belief formation even though they are usually automatic processes and therefore seem more passive than they really are, more like things that happen to us than like things we do. That the toothbrusher is not necessitated to select the red brush even though she always does so seems obvious enough. Thus her action, although so habitual as to be automatic, is sufficiently close to voluntary action under conditions of choice as to be reasonably classifiable with the latter. I am not of course contending that seeing and believing should be classified as *actions*, but merely that, like habitual behavior, they are quasi-voluntary uses of our bodies, more like things we do than like things that just happen to us. We don't absolutely have to see what we don't want to see—we can refuse to look, or to focus—nor believe what we don't want to believe, as the pervasive phenomenon of self-deception demonstrates.

Do we choose our feelings and emotions? The question sounds silly. Who can help feeling pleasure or pain, anger or pity, pride or shame? We may try to stimulate or suppress our emotions and feelings by various devices that cause their arousal or subsidence. But surely we cannot produce in ourselves feelings and emotions by mere self-command, other than, perhaps, the pseudo-emotions of the actor. How then, if use implies purpose and purpose implies possible choice, can feelings and emotions be uses we make of our bodies? Feeling pain, for example, is hardly something that we can be said to do and decide not to do. Yet I believe that something like my toothbrushing example is at work here, although more subtly.

Consider a slight injury, say a gentle pinch or bite. If the sensation has a favorable significance to us, if, say, the pinch or bite is experienced as the playful nip of one's lover or one's child, then it is experienced as pleasant. But suppose one suddenly realizes that the bite he thought was from his lover was actually the bite of a tarantula. His pleasure would immediately turn into pain. It might be said that this evidence of some room for choice between pleasure and pain is true only for weak stimuli. A knife in the gut, even if wielded by one's lover, could hardly be experienced as anything but painful. Trotsky wrote in his history of the Russian Revolution that people may be free to respond variably to the prick of a pin, but not to the touch of a red-hot iron. But consider that in dramatic emergencies such as a battle or an automobile collision, people often sustain grievous wounds without at the moment feeling pain. There is a neurological explanation of this phenomenon, stated effectively by Dennett, to the effect that energy is shunted from the pain center of the brain to the motor center, for purposes of action. Now who shunts the energy, if not the agent? So isn't that, at least, something she can be said to do, even if she isn't aware of doing it, and does for the purposes of self-preservation and assistance to others? As in the toothbrushing case, this is not clearly a voluntary response, because there appear no alternatives worth considering, but, if there *were* a conspicuous alternative, the agent might respond differently. For example, the coward, on sustaining a wound, might collapse while the wounded hero surges forward.

I am suggesting that perceiving, feeling, and believing, as well as reasoning, imagining, and acting, are uses that we make of our bodies, for the reason that they are all processes that are not causally determined in advance of their occurrence; we have some degree of choice of response even when our responses are automatic, for, unlike machines, when we see a good reason to respond otherwise, we do.

I have taken the hard cases first. That deliberation, discourse, and overt action are uses we make of our bodies seems beyond dispute, and thus requires no argumentative support. So let us now apply these considerations to the mind-body problem.

C. D. Broad and others have argued that, on a roughly Humean view of causality (I say "roughly" because Broad thinks it likely that causality involves something more than mere constant conjunction), there is no good reason to find mind-body interaction perplexing. As Broad put it, no two things could have less in common than drafts and head colds, yet no one doubts that the one can cause the other. His example was not the best choice, since drafts and head colds are physical states of lowered temperature and thus have quite a lot in common. But his main point, that constant conjunctions can conceivably hold between totally dissimilar things, can be granted. Like Hume, Broad thought that this fact supports determinism because, like Hume, he assumed a unitary, deterministic sense of "cause." But once a distinction is made between two senses of "cause," it is clear that the sense that applies to a given constant conjunction need not be the deterministic, dyadic sense.

There can be no doubt that two things that have nothing in common can regularly succeed each other over a long interval of time. During any length of time you like, it is possible that every winner at a certain gambling table wore white, either because such attire was required, or as a matter of sheer coincidence, or because after several white-clothed gamblers won at that table, subsequent gamblers superstitiously donned similar attire. In the last case, we would say that the fact that some white-attired gamblers won caused the others to wear white, rather than that wearing white was directly (dyadically) the cause of winning. The former use of "caused," unlike the latter, doesn't sound deterministic. The subsequent, superstitious gamblers were free to defy superstition but chose not to. At least, this seems a natural way to describe the matter.

But I am not suggesting that psychological causation is mere fortuitous coincidence. As Davidson has remarked, the "because" in "X did A because X wanted to achieve B" has a non-random ring to it. I wish only to make the rather trite point that constant conjunctions, by themselves, do not engender the disbelief and perplexity that infect the mind-body problem, and then to raise the question: Why not? I suggest that it is the insistence on a *necessary connection* between mental and bodily process that engenders the sense of an impenetrable mystery. The problem is not really, How can it be that certain bodily actions regularly follow certain mental states or vice versa? but rather, How can the one *make* the other happen? How, for example, can thirst make me drink, or hunger make me eat?

The answer, I suggest, is they can't. We often don't eat when we are hungry because we have some reason to refrain. Hunger is a good reason to eat, but one may also have a good reason to refrain, if the food is poisoned or belongs to someone else, or if one is on a diet or a hunger strike or a religious fast. The perplexity occasioned by the classical mind-body problem is due to the inconsistency of believing that there are irreducibly mental processes and also believing that they are deterministically related to bodily processes. Deny the first as reductive materialists do and the perplexity disappears, but the mind disappears with it. Deny the second, and the perplexity alone disappears. Which trick is more impressive? Kant thought to answer Hume's skeptical challenge to the belief in necessary causal connections by proposing that the principle of universal causation is imposed on experience by our innate categories rather than gleaned from experience. Critics of Kant have pointed out that this theory, even if it were true, would still fail to explain how we know that only *some* constant conjunctions are causally necessary while others are not. It explains perhaps why we always look for necessary connections but not why we do not always find them. I have no ambition to rush in where angels have tried but failed, so I shall not offer a criterion of necessary connection, such as deducibility from laws or from a unifying theory. I want merely to suggest why it is that we sometimes feel that one explanation has succeeded in revealing a necessary connection and another has not, why, in particular, mechanistic explanations satisfy us in this manner and psychological explanations don't.

It is a historical cliché that the science of mechanics, founded by Galileo and elevated to its zenith by Newton, has ever since served as a model for scientific theories. Why is mechanics so favored? I suggest that it is so favored because it explains events in terms of an underlying process of transference of a fundamental property, such as momentum, on contact between two objects, and that the paradigm case of this process, which makes it so compellingly believable, is one object pushing or pulling another. Later developments in physics did not quite meet this condition. Gravitation, electromagnetic induction, and, most dramatically, quantum mechanics retained something basic to mechanistic explanation, namely, the paradigm process of transfer of *some* conserved property, such as mass-energy from one part of space to an adjacent part. Without claiming insight into the history of science, I think it safe to say that an explanation still satisfies us as revealing causal necessity only when it describes an underlying process linking observable cause with observable effect in some way that, even if it does not exactly fit the push-pull paradigm, at least resembles it—in brief, when the explanation describes a *mechanism* at work. It is the revelation of a connecting mechanism that convinces us of the *necessity* of a constant conjunction of alleged cause and effect.

Now contrast the push-pull paradigm of mechanistic causality with the simplest paradigm of psychological causality, such as feeling thirsty and drinking, or deciding to turn on the light and then doing so. No one in his right mind would take these examples as *paradigms* of causal necessity. Determinists would of course argue that they are really, if not obviously, cases of causal necessity, and this would become clear if we could find the underlying mechanisms at work, but the need to *find* such mechanisms is enough to show that these cases are not *paradigms* of causal necessity but, on the contrary, need to be supplanted by deeper-level explanations that reduce them to a mechanistic paradigm.

Freud attempted to provide such deeper-level explanations and so did behavioral psychologists such as B. F. Skinner, although Skinner got no further than analogies to rats and pigeons. Freud's deeper-level explanations of abnormal psychological phenomena were interestingly two-layered. On the upper basement level of the unconscious he offered genuinely psychological explanations in terms of repressed purposes, so as to show that apparently involuntary behavior, like slips of the tongue, dreams, and hysterical symptoms, were voluntary after all, that is, that they satisfied, on an unconscious level, the simple paradigms of purposive behavior like drinking when one is thirsty. But on the sub-basement level, he introduced mechanistic concepts like cathexis and libido in an attempt to reduce his upper-level explanations to mechanistic ones employing hydrodynamic paradigms, whereupon he concluded that psychology had become as rigorously scientific as chemistry, not realizing that if he were right, it would have ceased to be psychology and become applied physiology.

Assuming that mental events and processes are uses we make of our bodies, how are they indeterministically related to physical stimuli and motor responses? This is what remains of the classical mind-body problem and it is no longer inscrutably mysterious. Bombardment of our sense organs by physical stimuli provides us with *reasons* to perceive, feel, and think as we do. To borrow an apt term from Malebranche, stimuli *occasion* mental responses, and these in turn occasion overt actions, in the sense of providing reasons for selecting means to ends. How then does one's mind make one's body do what one decides to do? This is the wrong question. There is no direct making involved in the transactions between mind and body: one is not the slave or puppet of the other; rather, both are tools of the person who owns them. There are, of course, internal physiological processes between the central nervous system and the sense organs and musculature that constitute deterministic causal chains, but these chains, taken as a whole, make up our simple or basic actions, the things we do without having to do something else to bring them about, so that the question of how we do them gets no purchase. On the level of action, "how?" means "by what procedure?" not "by what deterministic causal process?" To insist that "how" must mean the latter is to beg the question in favor of reductionism. Not that we can always do whatever we want. There are necessary physiological conditions for performing voluntary actions, the absence of which explains failure, but the mere presence of which cannot explain voluntary doing. Given the necessary physiological conditions, the only sufficient condition for performing a voluntary action is—doing it. For if there were some other sufficient condition, then the production of *that* condition, rather than the action thereby generated, would be the action in question.

How then does the body affect the mind and the mind affect the body? Bodily and mental stimuli provide the agent with reasons to think, feel, and act, and allow for alternative responses. No problem remains of how a mental event *makes* a bodily event occur or vice versa. It doesn't: The proper paradigm is the thirst-drink, not the push-pull, paradigm. The stimulus occasions, prompts, elicits the agent's response; it does not necessitate it. It is the agent who responds, not the stimulus that produces the response as if the agent had nothing to do with the matter. That is why causing someone to do something is a metaphysical gulf apart from plain causing. And that is why the causal relation between stimulus and response is triadic, that is, mediated by the agent, and indeterministic, depending as it does on the agent's momentary assessment of reasons, and thus allowing for alternative responses to exactly the same stimulus conditions.

Suppose I declare, "Well, that's it. The mind-body problem has been solved. Mind and body affect each other indirectly through the agent and therefore indeterministically, so no underlying mechanism need be or can be found to explain how such different entities can be related by causal laws—they aren't." No one will be impressed by that declaration. The reader will have a vague but insistent feeling that there's more to the problem than the mere issue of determinism versus indeterminism, and the reader will be right. But I don't think there is more to the problem of how *interaction* is possible, which is the Cartesian mind-body problem. A different but related problem remains that is easily conflated with the problem of interaction, namely, the status of the agent through whom the interaction is mediated, that is, the person. If a person just is a body, or some part of it, such as the brain, then whatever can be predicated of a person can be predicated of her body or brain. But then the body or brain must have mental predicates, or else mental predicates must be reducible to physical predicates as reductionists claim. The realization that neither of these conclusions is palatable then seems to drive us back toward the position of Cartesian dualism, that a person is identical with her mind and that the mind is a subject of mental predicates only. And this position engenders the interaction problem: How, if mind has no physical predicates, can it interact with body, which has no mental predicates?

Mind and Person

But the position I have proposed does not require us to think of mind as an immaterial substance, that is, as a *subject* of mental predicates. We can rather think of mind as a family of mental predicates whose subject or owner is also the owner of bodily predicates, namely, the person. What then is a person, if neither a body nor a mind, but something that *has* both body and mind? Is it a substance, and, if so, is it a third kind of substance, neither material nor mental, in which case, what kind of predicates is *it* the subject of? The answers must be, I think, that to say a person has both a mind and a body means precisely that a person has both physical and mental features and is therefore, in a sense, a "third" substance, neither purely mental nor purely physical, but both. I say, "in a sense a third substance," because on this view, neither mind nor body is really a substance, since they are *not* the ultimate subjects of mental or of bodily predicates. The person is the subject of both, so in reality, there is only one substance at issue here: the person. Strawson, in his early book, *Individuals*, wrongly considered bodies to be a different type of substance from persons, misled, I think, by the ambiguity of the term "body," which, when it serves as a synonym for material object, does denote a proper subject, but not when it serves to designate the physical parts and features of a person.

But then what is this strange (yet really not so strange) entity, a person, who is neither a mind nor a body but is the owner of both? Is it a disembodied (and perhaps also disminded) soul, a non-physical (and why not non-mental) ghost of a ghost that occupies and controls an organic body for a while? Derek Parfit seems to think this absurdity is the only alternative to identifying a person either with its body (which, for good reasons, Parfit rejects) or with a stream of unowned experiences (which, for reasons not as good, he accepts). He refuses to countenance the alternative that a person is necessarily the owner of both a mind *and* a body and cannot exist without either one. But, it might be protested, how can I claim that a person owns and uses her body if she cannot exist without it? Must she not be identical with it? I think not. There are other cases of an X that cannot exist without a Y although X has a Y and uses it. For example, a nation and its citizenry, a team and its members, a company and its employees. Nation, team, and company, it is true, are more abstract entities than persons, so that many philosophers insist, for good reasons, on their reducibility to their constituent citizens, members, or stockholders, and tolerate them only as convenient fictions. Susan Wolf has pointed out that even these rather abstract entities are not entirely reducible to their constituent individuals, because they involve institutional relations of authority, responsibility, and so on. But I would concede to the positivists that such entities are, in an important way, less irreducibly real than persons, for at least two reasons: (1) When nations, teams, and companies can be said to do something, it is their citizens, members, or employees and stockholders who do it. Not so for persons. When you light a match it is really you that lights it, not your hand or your brain. (2) Although nations and so on cannot exist without their constituents, their constituents can very well exist without them, not, of course, in their capacity as constituents, but in other capacities. But minds cannot exist in any capacity without persons who own them. Bodies, it is true (and this may be the main argument in favor of materialism), can outlast their owners, in somewhat the way employees can outlast the company that employs them, that is, in a different capacity. But a body without a person is a corpse, a lump of protoplasm, no longer a living human body. A corpse is indeed a material substance, a subject of physical properties such as weight, size, and shape. But unlike an unemployed worker, it no longer has the properties of a human agent, such as strength or weakness, quickness or lethargy, grace or clumsiness, durability or fragility. So there is some asymmetry between mind and body that weighs somewhat in favor of materialism over dualism, but not enough to justify reducing a person to its body, for that would eliminate the subject of human predicates. Persons, unlike nations, teams, and corporations are indispensable subjects of mental predicates, bodily predicates, and action descriptions. And that is as it should be. Persons, after all, are where the action is.

NOTES

Preface

1. Plato, *Phaedo*, trans. H. Tredennick, in *Collected Dialogues of Plato*, ed. E. Hamilton and D. Cairns (Princeton, N.J.: Princeton University Press, 1961), 98d–98e, p. 80.

Chapter 1

1. Ludwig Wittgenstein, *Philosophical Investigations*, trans. G. E. M. Anscombe (London: Macmillan, 1953), para. 621.

2. Some would say that at least the image of the bone in the water exists and causes the dog's response. But it can only do so if the dog takes it to be a real bone. Thus it is the taking, not the image, that has causal efficacy, and the taking is independent of the existence of the bone (and even of the image). Some would say that this "taking" is an event, and is the real cause of the dog's response, but I doubt if the taking can be distinguished from the response it is alleged to cause. See Chapter 2, on decisions.

3. Peter Unger suggested to me that my triadic-dyadic distinction sounds too formal and does not bring out the essence of the difference between psychological and physical causality. Very well. In what follows, the reader can mentally substitute "agent-mediated" wherever I say "triadic," and the point will be clear.

4. By "simultaneous," I do *not* mean that the operative or effective decision, as contrasted with the provisional or, as Donald Davidson would say, *prima facie* decision, is an event that can be dated or clocked. Perhaps, as William Ruddick has suggested to me, the temporal adjective "simultaneous" is misleading in this regard. I shall argue in Chapter 2 that

decisions, choices, intentions, volitions, undertakings, and so on are not events, but aspects or features of actions, and that they consist in the agent's being able to do otherwise and being, in one way or another, aware of what he is doing. See Chapter 2.

Chapter 2

1. Joseph Butler, "Of Personal Identity," in *Works,* ed. S. Halifax (London: Oxford University Press, 1849); Thomas Reid, *Essays on the Active Powers of Man,* in *Works,* ed. J. Dugal (Charleston: Etheridge, 1813); Roderick Chisholm, "Freedom and Action," in *Freedom and Determinism,* ed. K. Lehrer (New York: Random House, 1966), pp. 11–44.

2. David Lewis, "Survival and Identity," *Philosophical Papers,* vol. 1 (London: Oxford University Press, 1983); Derek Parfit, *Reasons and Persons* (London: Oxford University Press, 1984), pt. 2.

3. P. F. Strawson, "Freedom and Resentment," in *Philosophy of Thought and Action,* ed. P. F. Strawson (London: Oxford University Press, 1968).

4. David M. Armstrong, *A Materialist Theory of the Mind* (London: Routledge and Kegan Paul, 1968).

5. Baruch Spinoza, *Ethics,* trans. R. Elwes (New York: Dover, 1955), pts. 4 and 5; Paul d'Holbach, *System of Nature,* trans. H. Robinson (New York: Burt Franklin, 1795), chap. 11; John Hospers, "What Means This Freedom?" in *Determinism and Freedom in an Age of Modern Science,* ed. Sidney Hook (New York: Colliers, 1961), pp. 126–142; Paul Edwards, "Hard and Soft Determinism," in *Determinism and Freedom,* ed. Hook, pp. 117–125; J. J. C. Smart, *Philosophy and Scientific Realism* (New York: Humanities Press, 1963); Parfit, *Reasons and Persons,* chaps. 15 and 20.

6. Abraham I. Melden, *Free Action* (New York: Humanities Press, 1961), p. 201: "Does the rejection of the causal model imply that . . . freedom is to be purchased at the expense of a capricious indeterminism?" See

also Thomas Nagel, *The View from Nowhere* (London: Oxford University Press, 1986), chap. 7. In *What Does It All Mean* (London: Oxford University Press, 1987), pp. 54–56, Nagel says: "If we think that what he did was determined in advance, this seems more like punishing a dog for chewing on the rug. . . . I myself don't think it makes sense to blame someone for doing what it was imposssible for him not to do. . . . But the problem is, if the act wasn't determined in advance, by your desires, beliefs and personality, among other things, it seems to be something that just happened, without any explanation. And in that case, how was it *your* doing?"

7. Henry Frankfurt, "Alternative Possibilities and Moral Responsibility," *Journal of Philosophy* 66 (1969): 829–839.

8. David Wiggins, "Towards a Reasonable Libertarianism," in *Essays on Freedom of Action,* ed. T. Honderich (London: Routledge and Kegan Paul, 1973), pp. 31–62.

9. C. A. Campbell, *On Selfhood and Godhood* (London: Allen and Unwin, 1957), lec. 9. In "Freedom and Action," pp. 11–14, Chisholm says: "The point is, in a word, that whenever a man does something, A, then (by immanent causation) he makes a certain cerebral event happen and this cerebral event (by transeunt causation) makes A happen." It may be that all Chisholm means by his mysterious sounding "immanent causation" is what I am calling agent-mediated causality, but if, like Butler and Reid, whom he cites with favor, he means something more metaphysical, something like substantial causation, as a dyadic relation between agent and either brain event or action, then I can't make sense of the notion. If the agent is the substantial cause of A, then why isn't she always A'ing? Is there some trigger cause that sets off the A'ing? Then we are back in both the dilemma and the regress. The same problem arises in his later book, *Person and Object* (London: Allen and Unwin, 1976), chap. 3.

10. Peter van Inwagen, *Essay on Free Will* (Oxford: Clarendon, 1983); Richard Peters, *The Concept of Motivation* (New York: Humanities Press, 1968); Anthony Kenny, *Free Will and Responsibility* (London: Routledge-and Kegan Paul, 1978); John Lucas, *The Freedom of the Will* (Oxford: Clarendon, 1970).

11. Stephen Stich, *From Folk Psychology to Cognitive Science* (Cambridge, Mass.: MIT Press, 1983); Myles Brand, *Intending and Acting* (Cambridge, Mass.: MIT Press, 1984); Paul Churchland, *Matter and Consciousness* (Cambridge, Mass.: MIT Press, 1984).

12. Gilbert Ryle, *The Concept of Mind* (New York: Barnes and Noble, 1949).

13. Cf. Henry W. Johnstone, *The Problem of Self* (University Park: Pennsylvania State University Press, 1970).

14. If, like Martin Buber, you think we ought to say "thou" to trees and rocks, then you don't think we should ever adopt the objective attitude toward anything.

15. Strawson, "Freedom and Resentment," p. 16. See Chapter 9, below.

16. Strawson, "Freedom and Resentment," p. 88.

17. Galen Strawson, *Freedom and Belief* (Oxford: Clarendon, 1986). Strawson argues that the M-N dilemma holds on both levels, that of first-order decision to act, and that of second-order evaluation of first-order desires and decisions. He therefore argues for impalement on the determinist horn by abandoning the belief in what he calls "self determination and true responsibility," as irremediably inconsistent with what he calls, a bit tendentiously, "our belief in the unity of truth" (pp. 25, 46–55, 314–317).

What leads Strawson to consider the dilemma irremediable on both levels is his assumption that all causal explanation (or, in his terms, "rational explanation," which, he says, need not be causal) is deterministic in the sense that it states the conditions that "decisively shape" the explicandum, in this case a voluntary action. He does not consider the possibility that an action A might be completely explained by a reason R, and an alternative action B equally completely explainable by a different reason R', where the only difference that makes the first explanation appropriate and the second worthless is that the agent decided to do A, not B. Luther decided to break with the Church of Rome in order to uphold the principle of *sole fide,* rather than compromise in order to avoid a violent conflict. Galen Strawson, Thomas Nagel, and others who believe the dilemma is irremediable would probably insist that, if Luther's decision was rational, there must be an additional reason R″ that explains his second-order decision to decide to act on R rather than on R′. (Cf. Nagel, *The View from Nowhere,* p. 123.)

Strawson perceives that this demand leads to an infinite regress, but he thinks this problem arises only for the libertarian who insists on the "self-determination" of desire. He does not notice that the regress is just as infinite for the determinist (Davidson does notice it) because what remains absent from this picture on any level is the trigger event. Even if one had no need to choose between R and R′, because one was totally committed to the priority of R, so that R fully explains one's doing A, R still does not explain why one does A at one moment rather than another, why, for example, Luther did not moderate his language at the Diet of Worms (a wonderfully appropriate name!), postponing his break for a more propitious time, or even forever. To use Galen Strawson's own terminology, reasons alone, since they are dispositions rather than occurrences, cannot "decisively shape" a voluntary action but need a trigger event to actualize them. A second-order decision to decide to do A is no more a trigger event than is a first-order decision to do A, for the reasons I gave earlier. So if we keep on looking for a trigger decision, we shall have to climb the ladder unendingly, whether that trigger event be one of self-determination or one of determination by external causes. The escape I suggest is to stop looking, by recognizing that, on any level, decision is not an event, but simply the knowing exercise of the ability to do or not to do.

Davidson recognizes this trigger problem presented by his own dispositional account of a primary reason as the cause of a voluntary action, and offers a solution that will not, I think, stand the strain: "The antecedent condition is prior to and separate from the action, and so is suited to be a cause (in this case, it is a state rather than an event, but this could be changed along these lines: 'coming to have desires and beliefs that rationalize x')" (Donald Davidson, "Freedom to Act," in *Essays on Actions and Events* [London: Oxford University Press, 1980], p. 73.

This suggestion won't do the job, because the event of coming to have a desire or a belief could only, at best, produce the disposition to perform action x, not x itself, or else x is merely a non-voluntary reflex rather than an intentional action. The missing condition is the operative decision to do x, a decision that Davidson astutely recognizes is *not* an independent event, and thus cannot qualify as a trigger cause: "In order to be eligible as a cause, the event mentioned must be separate from the action. . . . The objection applies to choosing, willing, intending and trying. None of these is plausibly the cause of an action because normally these are ways of characterizing the action chosen, willed, intended or tried, not descriptions of further actions, events or states" (*ibid.*, p. 72).

Davidson is on the right track here, but he doesn't seem to realize that this feature, decision, choice, intention, or attempt, which marks the action as voluntary, would be short-circuited by his dyadic causal theory of primary reasons directly causing actions. He is right in perceiving that these features are not trigger events, but he fails to see that his candidate for the trigger cause, namely, "coming to believe or desire," would doom decisions, choices, and so on to epiphenomenal vacuity.

18. Daniel Dennett, *Brainstorms: Philosophical Essays on Mind and Psychology* (Montgomery, Vt.: Bradford Books, 1978), chap. 15, pp. 286–299, and *Elbow Room* (Cambridge, Mass.: MIT Press, 1984), pp. 123–155.

19. Although this is an important feature of decision-making that, he is right to point out, has considerable survival value in enabling us to escape the predicament of Buridan's ass, who starved to death due to the inability to make an arbitrary decision.

20. Dennett, *Elbow Room*, p. 133.

21. Henry Frankfurt, "Freedom of the Will and the Concept of a Person," *Journal of Philosophy* 68 (1971): 5–20.

22. Dennett, *Elbow Room*, p. 142, n. 8.

23. Hospers, "What Means This Freedom?"

24. In Chapter 1, I stated briefly the reason why I do not consider decisions that are not merely provisional or *prima facie* to be events of any kind. Perhaps I should flesh out the argument here, since it is crucial to the issue at stake. First, I should explain more fully my use of the term "decision." I

am employing it as a generic term to cover the ordinary use of "decision" but also that of "intention," "choice," "volition," Chisholm's "undertaking," the legalistic *mens rea,* and whatever mental set is sufficient for a voluntary action, given all the necessary environmental and internal physiological and mental states of the agent. We do not to my knowledge have a term in everyday language that does so general a job. I suspect there is a good reason we don't, namely, that there is no actual process required for the voluntariness of action (as Anthony Kenny has noted), but only the fact that the agent could do otherwise and is aware of what he or she does. In any case, in the absence of a commonly used generic term, I shall take the liberty of using "decision" in this way. Davidson employs "intention" for the same purpose, as do others such as Myles Brand, but as Davidson himself observes, "intention" is a forward-looking word, suggestive of later action, and thus not really appropriate for a feature of the action itself. The lack of a good generic term may be a reason why earlier philosophers talked of acts of will, volitions, and even "volitings," and why Campbell insists that only mental acts are fully voluntary, since the bodily movements that normally result from the mental act of willing do not always result, and are thus, for him, only contingently related to their mental cause.

It was on reading Davidson that I first came to suspect that decisions are not events, and my brief argument to that effect in Chapter 1 was inspired by the passage in Davidson quoted earlier, in note 18.

Davidson, however, clings to the belief that intentions, decisions, and so on are mental events of *some* kind, a belief that I propose we abandon in favor of regarding these notions simply as ways of indicating voluntariness. He wants them to be events because he wants to hold on to determinism, but he realizes that they cannot be dated or clocked. In a later paper, "Intending," in *Essays on Actions and Events,* he argues that intentions are a species of practical judgment: "In the case of pure intending, I now suggest that the intention simply is an all-out judgment. . . . An intention cannot single out a particular action in an intelligible sense, since it is directed to the future. . . . But there is nothing absurd in my judging that any action of mine in the immediate future that is the eating of something sweet would be desireable given the rest of what I believe about the immediate future." And he writes: "In the case of intentional action, at least when the action is of brief duration, nothing seems to stand in the way of an Aristotelian identification of the action with a judgment of a certain kind—an all-out, unconditional judgment that the action is desireable" (p. 99).

So an operative (not merely provisional) intention is a judgment—but it is also the action intended. Thus is a maiden sawed in two yet left intact. I suggest we accept Davidson's identification of the operative intention with the action intended and forget about the all-out practical judgment, which is, after all, the same old voluntary action in a more intellectual dress.

Davidson is desperately looking for a trigger cause of action. He takes note of the problem that primary reasons (desires and beliefs) are dispositions and so need a trigger to activate them, and he claims to find the trigger in "coming to have" the desires and beliefs. The suggestion is borne of desperation, a straw that cannot keep determinism afloat. For we can ask: How long does the coming to believe or desire take, in order to bring about the action x? Is it clockable? If so, why is it not merely provisional before the action takes place, and how does it change from provisional to operative? If not, then in what sense is it a process of becoming? Recall the scenes in Shakespeare's *Julius Caesar* in which Cassius and Brutus, defeated on the battlefield, beg their lieutenants to kill them. Cassius' lieutenant obeys, and then flees in fear of punishment by the victors, while Brutus' lieutenant agrees only to hold the sword for Brutus to impale himself upon, and is later honored for his doing so. Why the difference, if not because, until one acts, one's intention or decision is provisional and subject to retraction? For example, Brutus might, at the last split second, have swerved from the sword point. Cassius, however, was (literally) stuck.

There may be something more to an operative decision than mere ability to do otherwise together with awareness of what one is doing, but if a seeker with the prescience of Davidson cannot successfully find it, I am not going to try.

25. Edward Sankowski, "Freedom, Determinism and Character," *Mind* 89 (1980): 106–113: "There are, in the region of discourse about character, locutions involving necessity which certainly do not rule out freedom. . . . Consider locutions like the following: 'He had to do that,' 'It was a necessity for him to do what he believes in,' 'He could do no other given his nature,' 'I must do this.' . . . In this sense, a full explication of the idea of freedom seems to require reference to necessity of a sort." Does it indeed? And if I say, as I climb into your window and point a revolver at you, "Circumstances and my character necessitate my shooting you and taking your valuables," will you take me literally and not even *try* to talk me out of it?

Gary Watson has argued that we might well be determined by our valuational system, and still be free and responsible (in "Free Agency," *Journal of Philsophy* 83 [1986]: 517–521). But this claim seems to me inconsistent with his rejection of acculturation as a source of freely motivated action. For what if, which seems likely, the agent's valuational system is itself the product of acculturation? Watson's examples of reduced responsibility seem to me only to illustrate cases of conflict between deep-rooted attitudes and present judgment. But what if there is no conflict, because the agent just automatically follows tradition? Does that make the agent *more* free and responsible? Mustn't the agent be free to accept or reject, decide in favor of or against either acculturation or native tradition, if she is to be held responsible for her conduct? And can she not, on the second-order level of reflection, decide in favor of or against her overall valuational system, as seems to happen in cases of sudden conversion (cf. the next chapter)?

26. C. A. Campbell, "Is Free Will a Pseudo Problem?" *Mind* 60 (1951): 446–455.

Chapter 3

1. Peter van Inwagen, *Essay on Free Will* (Oxford: Clarendon, 1983), pp. 94, 222.

2. Kurt Baier, "Responsibility and Action," in *The Nature of Human Action,* ed. Myles Brand (Glenview, Ill.: Scott Foresman, 1970), pp. 100–116.

3. *Ibid.,* pp. 103–108; Jonathan Glover, *Responsibility* (New York: Humanities Press, 1978); Herbert Fingarette, *On Responsibility* (New York: Basic Books, 1967).

4. Edward Sankowski, "Freedom, Determinism and Character," *Mind* 89 (1980): 106–113.

5. R. B. Hobart, "Free Will as Involving Determination and Inconceivable Without It," *Mind* 43 (1934): 1–27; J. J. C. Smart, *Utilitarianism: For and Against* (Cambridge, Eng.: Cambridge University Press, 1973), sec. 10; Daniel Dennett, *Elbow Room* (Cambridge, Mass.: MIT Press, 1984), pp. 159–172.

Chapter 4

1. Luke 15: 11–31, *The New American Bible* (Washington, D.C.: Catholic University Press, 1970).

2. "The parable is primarily a recognition of the forgiving quality of God's mercy and love" *The Interpreter's Dictionary of the Bible,* ed. G. A. Buttrick [New York: Abingdon Press, 1962], vol. 3, p. 654).

3. Cf. G. A. Buttrick, *The Parables of Jesus* (Garden City, N.Y.: Doubleday, 1928); A. T. Cadoux, *The Parables of Jesus* (Garden City, N.Y.: Doubleday, 1928); C. H. Dodd, *The Parables of the Kingdom* (London: Nisbet, 1936); W. O. E. Oesterley, *The Gospel Parables in the Light of Their Jewish Background* (New York: Macmillan, 1936).

4. Archbishop R. O. Trent, *Notes on the Parables of Our Lord* (New York: Appleton, 1880).

5. C. A. Campbell, "The Psychology of Effort of the Will," *Proceedings of the Aristotelian Society* 64 (1940): 49–74. Campbell fails to distinguish efforts of the will, which may be morally neutral or self-serving, from specifically moral effort.

6. J. S. Mill, *An Examination of Sir William Hamilton's Philosophy*, reprinted in *Free Will and Determinism*, ed. Bernard Berofsky (New York: Harper and Row, 1966), pp. 159–174.

7. Henry Frankfurt, "Freedom of the Will and the Concept of a Person," *Journal of Philosophy* 68 (1971): 5–20.

8. See my *Persons: A Study in Philosophical Psychology* (London: Macmillan, 1977), chap. 4.

9. Thomas Nagel, "Moral Luck," in *Mortal Questions* (Cambridge, Eng.: Cambridge University Press, 1979), chap. 3; B. A. O. Williams, "Moral Luck," *Proceedings of the Aristotelian Society*, supp. vol. 50 (1976): 115–135.

Chapter 5

1. H. J. Eysenck, *Uses and Abuses of Psychology* (London and Baltimore: Penguin Books, 1953), pp. 195–198.

2. Gilbert Ryle, *The Concept of Mind* (New York: Barnes and Noble, 1949), chap. 1.

3. Plato, *Protagoras*, trans. Benjamin Jowett (London: Oxford University Press, 1871), 316b–332d.

4. Aristotle, *Nichomachean Ethics*, trans. W. D. Ross (New York: Modern Library, 1947), 1095a.

5. Jean-Paul Sartre, *Being and Nothingness: An Essay on Phenomenological Ontology*, trans. Hazel E. Barnes (New York: Pocket Books, 1966), pt. 1, chap. 2.

6. Philip Rieff, *Freud: The Mind of the Moralist* (New York: Anchor, 1961), pp. 278–280.

7. Joseph Margolis, *Psychotherapy and Morality* (New York: Random House, 1966), pp. 108–109.

8. *Ibid.*, p. 110.

9. *Ibid.*, p. 111.

10. R. D. Laing, *The Politics of Experience* (New York: Ballantine, 1968).

11. Rollo May, *Love and Will* (New York: Norton, 1969).

12. J. H. Van den Berg, *A Different Existence* (Pittsburgh: Duquesne University Press, 1972).

13. Albert Ellis, *Reason and Emotion in Psychotherapy* (New York: L. S. Stuart, 1962).

14. Thomas Szasz, *The Myth of Mental Illness* (New York: Hoeber-Harper, 1961).

15. Edward F. Torrey, *The Death of Psychiatry* (Radnor, Pa.: Chilton, 1974).

16. Roy Schafer, "Action: Its Place in Psychoanalytic Interpretation and Theory," *Annual of Psychoanalysis* 1 (1973): 159–196.

Chapter 6

1. David Abrahamson, *The Psychology of Crime* (New York: Columbia University Press, 1960); J. Wiggins and E. Schoeck, eds., *Psychiatry and Responsibility* (Princeton, N.J.: Van Nostrand, 1960).

2. Thomas Szasz, *The Myth of Mental Illness* (New York: Hoeber-Harper, 1961).

3. R. D. Laing, *The Politics of Experience* (New York: Ballantine, 1968); Edward F. Torrey, *The Death of Psychiatry* (Radnor, Pa.: Chilton, 1974).

4. Szasz, *The Myth of Mental Illness*.

5. Thomas Szasz, *The Manufacture of Madness* (New York: Harper, 1970).

6. Ken Kesey, *One Flew Over the Cuckoo's Nest* (New York: Viking, 1973).

7. Laing, *The Politics of Experience* and Torrey, *The Death of Psychiatry*, passim.

8. Jerry Rubin, *Growing (Up) at Thirty Seven* (New York: Evans, 1976).

9. Thomas Szasz, *The Ethics of Psychoanalysis* (New York: Basic Books, 1965), p. 32.

10. Torrey, *The Death of Psychiatry.*

Chapter 7

1. Cf. H. D. Thornburg, ed., *Contemporary Adolescence* (Belmont, Calif.: Wadsworth, 1971).

2. A. S. Alissi, "Concepts of Adolescence," in *Contemporary Adolescence*, ed. Thornburg, p. 31: "The meaning of eruption and turmoil during adolescence is important. Upset behavior is seen to be an external indication of internal adjustments taking place and these are taken to be signs of *normal* growth. Conversely, when there is a steady equilibrium during adolescence, there is abnormality."

3. For example, in the *New York Times* essay by Irving Kaufman, "The Insanity Plea on Trial," *New York Times Sunday Magazine*, Aug. 8, 1982, pp. 16–26, the distinguished judge assumes that any loss of control is adequate evidence of mental illness.

4. Cf. Thomas Szasz, *The Myth of Mental Illness* (New York: Hoeber-Harper, 1961); R. D. Laing, *The Politics of Experience* (New York: Ballantine, 1968); Edward F. Torrey, *The Death of Psychiatry* (Radnor, Pa.: Chilton, 1974).

5. Kaufman, "The Insanity Plea on Trial."

6. Arthur C. Danto, "Freedom and Forebearance," in *Freedom and Determinism*, ed. K. Lehrer (New York: Random House, 1966), pp. 60–63.

7. Arthur C. Danto, "Action, Knowledge and Representation," in *Action Theory*, ed. Myles Brand and D. Walton (Dordrecht: Reidel, 1976), pp. 11–26. For the defense of Danto's earlier view, cf. Roderick Chisholm, "The Agent as Cause," in the same volume.

8. Henry Frankfurt, "Freedom of the Will and the Concept of a Person," *Journal of Philosophy* 68 (1971): 5–20.

9. Cf. Alissi, "Concepts of Adolescence."

Chapter 8

1. Ludwig Wittgenstein, *The Blue and Brown Books,* ed. R. Rhees (Oxford: Blackwell, 1958).

2. Peter Winch, *The Idea of a Social Science* (London: Routledge and Kegan Paul, 1958).

3. A. R. Louch, *Explanation and Human Action* (Berkeley: University of California Press, 1966), pp. 174–182.

4. Richard Rudner, *Philosophy of Social Science* (Englewood Cliffs, N.J.: Prentice-Hall, 1966), p. 82.

5. *Ibid.,* p. 83.

6. Winch, *The Idea of a Social Science,* p. 47.

7. David Braybrooke, ed., *Philosophical Problems of the Social Sciences* (New York: Macmillan, 1965), p. 8.

8. *Ibid.,* p. 9.

9. *Ibid.,* p. 6.

10. *Ibid.*

11. Rudner, *Philosophy of Social Science,* p. 80.

Chapter 9

1. Joseph Weizenbaum, *Computer Power and Human Reason* (San Francisco: Freeman, 1976).

2. *Ibid.,* p. 227.

3. *Ibid.,* pp. 261–265.

4. Kenneth Sayre, *Consciousness: A Philosophic Study of Minds and Machines* (New York: Random House, 1969), p. 29.

5. *Ibid.*, p. 25.

6. *Ibid.*, p. 38.

7. *Ibid.*

8. Raziel Abelson, *Persons: A Study in Philosophical Psychology* (London: Macmillan, 1977).

9. Richard Rorty, "Mind-Body, Privacy and Categories," *Review of Metaphysics* 19 (1965); P. K. Feyerabend, "Materialism and the Mind-Body Problem," *Review of Metaphysics* 17 (1963).

10. Marvin Minsky, ed., *Semantic Information Processing* (Cambridge, Mass.: MIT Press, 1968), p. 12.

11. J. J. C. Smart, *Philosophy and Scientific Realism* (New York: Humanities Press, 1963), chap. 6.

12. Norman Malcolm, *Memory and Mind* (Ithaca, N.Y.: Cornell University Press, 1977), pp. 235–237.

Chapter 10

1. W. I. Matson, "Why Isn't the Mind-Body Problem Ancient?" in *Mind, Matter, and Method,* ed. P. K. Feyerabend and G. Maxwell (Minneapolis: University of Minnesota Press, 1966), p. 101.

2. John Searle, *Intentionality* (Cambridge, Eng.: Cambridge University Press, 1983), p. 15: "The 'mind-body problem' is no more real a problem than the 'stomach-digestion problem.' "

3. J. J. C. Smart, "Sensations and Brain Processes," *Philosophical Review* 67 (1959): 141–156.

4. Jerome Shaffer, "Mental Events and the Brain," *Journal of Philosophy* 60 (1963): 160–166; Joseph Cornman, "The Identity of Mind and Body," *Journal of Philosophy* 59 (1962): 476–492; Thomas Nagel, "Physicalism," *Philosophical Review* 74 (1965): 339–356.

5. Hilary Putnam, "Minds and Machines," in *Dimensions of Mind,* ed. Sidney Hook (New York: New York University Press, 1960), pp. 148–179; Jerry Fodor, *Psychological Explanation* (New York: Random House, 1968);

Daniell Dennett, *Brainstorms: Philosophical Essays on Mind and Psychology* (Montgomery, Vt.: Bradford Books, 1978), pp. 152–158.

6. Donald Davidson, "Freedom to Act," in *Essays on Actions and Events* (London: Oxford University Press, 1980), pp. 229–235. He calls his view "anomalous monism."

7. Arthur C. Danto, "Toward a Theory of Retentive Materialism," in *How Many Questions?: Essays in Honor of Sidney Morgenbesser,* ed. L. Cauman (Indianapolis: Hackett, 1983).

8. Smart, "Sensations and Brain Processes,"; David Lewis, "An Argument for the Identity Theory," in *Philosophical Papers,* vol. 1 (London: Oxford University Press, 1983): P. K. Feyerabend, "Mental Events and the Brains," *Journal of Philosophy* 60 (1963): 295–296; Richard Rorty, *Philosophy and the Mirror of Nature* (Princeton, N.J.: Princeton University Press, 1979), chaps. 1 and 2; Paul Churchland, *Scientific Realism and the Plasticity of Mind* (Cambridge, Eng.: Cambridge University Press, 1979), chap. 4. I am lumping together the strick identity views of Smart and Lewis with the eliminative materialism of Feyerabend, Rorty, and Churchland, because they agree on what concerns us here, the dispensability of "folk psychology."

9. Danto, "Toward a Theory of Retentive Materialism."

10. Dennett, *Brainstorms,* chap. 1.

11. Davidson, *Essays on Actions and Events,* essays 11 and 12.

12. *Ibid.,* p. 232.

13. *Ibid.,* p. 233.

14. *Ibid.,* p. 241.

15. Dennett, *Brainstorms,* p. 5.

16. Corman, "The Identity of Mind and Body," pp. 339–356: "For if, as Smart believes, all mental states are indeed brain processes, then when we have information about mental states we thereby have information about brain processes."

17. In criticizing identity theories I do not mean to defend any non-identity thesis like Cartesian substantial dualism. I do not, that is, mean to claim that a mental state or event is a different entity from any physical state

or event. It seems to me that the categorial gap between the mental and the physical is so wide that it makes no more sense either to affirm or to deny identities across the two categories than it would to affirm or deny that numbers are identical to numerals. Theoretical identity proponents like Cornman and Nagel have claimed that we can and do cross categories with identities like heat and mean kinetic energy of molecules, or lightning and electric discharge in the atmosphere, or color and electromagnetic waves of a certain frequency. But the categories involved in these identities are not as radically different as are the mental and the physical. I agree with the materialists (and, in this sense, I guess I *am* a materialist) that matter is the only stuff of which anything can be composed, if it is to be spatially-temporally locatable. People are composed of limbs and tissues as sculptures are composed of stone, wood, or metal, and nations of land and people. But the compositional relation is nothing like an identity relation, because it is non-symmetrical and it does not obey Leibniz' Law. Many writers have performed breathtaking calisthenics to surmount this obstacle to identity theory by defining weaker concepts of identity that evade Leibniz' Law. But the categorial gap remains and cannot be bridged by mere definitional stipulation, as Cornman himself remarked just before he tried to do it (Cornman, "The Identity of Mind and Body").

18. Putnam, "Minds and Machines."

BIBLIOGRAPHY

Abelson, Raziel. *Persons: A Study in Philosophical Psychology.* London: Macmillan, 1977.

Abrahamson, David. *The Psychology of Crime.* New York: Columbia University Press, 1960.

Alissi, A. S. "Concepts of Adolescence," In *Contemporary Adolescence,* ed. H. D. Thornburg, Belmont, Calif.: Wadsworth, 1971.

Aristotle. *Nichomachean Ethics,* trans. W. D. Ross, New York: Modern Library, 1947.

Armstrong, David M. *A Materialist Theory of the Mind.* London: Routledge and Kegan Paul, 1968.

Baier, Kurt. "Responsibility and Action," In *The Nature of Human Action,* ed. Myles Brand. Glenview, Ill.: Scott Foresman, 1970.

Berofsky, Bernard, ed. *Free Will and Determinism.* New York: Harper and Row, 1966.

Brand, Myles. *Intending and Acting.* Cambridge, Mass.: M. I. T. Press, 1984.

Braybrooke, David, ed. *Philosophical Problems of the Social Sciences.* New York: Macmillan, 1965.

Butler, Joseph. "Of Personal Identity," In *Works,* ed. S. Halifax, London: Oxford University Press, 1849.

Buttrick, G. A., ed. *The Interpreter's Dictionary of the Bible,* vol. 3. New York: Abingdon Press, 1962.

Cadoux, A. T. *The Parables of Jesus.* Garden City, N.Y.: Doubleday, 1982.

Campbell, C. A. *On Selfhood and Godhood.* London: Allen and Unwin, 1957.

——. "Is Free Will a Pseudo-Problem?" *Mind* 60 (1951).

——. "The Psychology of Efforts of the Will," *Proceedings of the Aristotelian Society* 60 (1940):49–74.

Chisholm, Roderick. "Freedom and Action," In *Freedom and Determinism.* New York: Random House, 1966.

———. *Person and Object.* London: Allen and Unwin, 1976.

Churchland, Paul. *Matter and Consciousness.* Cambridge, Mass.: M. I. T. Press, 1984.

———. *Scientific Realism and the Plasticity of Mind.* Cambridge, Eng.: Cambridge University Press, 1979.

Cornman, Joseph. "The Identity of Mind and Body," *Journal of Philosophy* 59, no. 18(1962).

Danto, Arthur C. "Action, Knowledge and Representation," In *Action Theory,* ed. Myles Brand and D. Walton. Dordrecht: Reidel, 1976.

———. "Freedom and Forebearance," In *Freedom and Determinism,* ed. K. Lehrer. New York: Random House, 1966.

———. "Toward a Theory of Retentive Materialism," In *How Many Questions?: Essays in Honor of Sidney Morgenbesser.* Indianapolis: Hackett, 1983.

Davidson, Donald. *Essays on Actions and Events.* London: Oxford University Press, 1980.

Dennett, Daniel. *Brainstorms: Philosophical Essays on Mind and Psychology.* Montgomery, Vt.: Bradford Books, 1978.

———. *Elbow Room.* Cambridge, Mass.: M. I. T. Press, 1984.

Dodd, C. H. *The Parables of the Kingdom.* London: Nisbet, 1936.

Edwards, Paul. "Hard and Soft Determinism," In *Determinism and Freedom in the Age of Modern Science,* ed. Sidney Hook. New York: Colliers, 1961.

Ellis, Albert. *Reason and Emotion in Psychotherapy.* New York: L. S. Stuart, 1962.

Eysenck, H. J. *Uses and Abuses of Psychology.* London and Baltimore: Penguin Books, 1953.

Feyerabend, P. K. "Materialism and the Mind-Body Problem," *Review of Metaphysics* 17 (1963).

———. "Mental Events and the Brain," *Journal of Philosophy* 60 (1963).

Fingarette, Herbert. *On Responsibility.* New York: Basic Books, 1967.

Fodor, Jerry. *Psychological Explanation.* New York: Random House, 1968.

Frankfurt, Henry. "Alternative Possibilities and Moral Responsibility," *Journal of Philosophy* 66 (1969):

———. "Freedon of Will and the Concept of a Person," *Journal of Philosophy* 68 (1971).

Glover, Jonathan. *Responsibility*. New York: Humanities Press, 1978.

Hobart, R. B. "Free Will as Involving Determinism and Inconceivable Without It," *Mind* 43 (1934).

D'Holbach, Paul. *System of Nature*. New York: Burt Franklin, 1975.

Hook, Sidney, ed. *Determinism and Freedom in the Age of Modern Science*. New York: Colliers, 1961.

Hospers, John. "What Means this Freedom?" In *Determinism and Freedom in the Age of Modern Science*, ed. Sidney Hook. New York: Colliers, 1961.

Johnstone, Henry W. *The Problem of the Self*. University Park, PA.: State University Press, 1970.

Kaufman, Irving. "The Insanity Plea on Trial," *New York Times Sunday Magazine*, Aug. 8, 1982.

Kenny, Anthony. *Free Will and Responsibility*. London: Routledge and Kegan Paul, 1978.

Kesey, Ken. *One Flew Over the Cuckoos Nest*. New York: Viking, 1973.

Laing, R. D. *The Politics of Experience*. New York: Ballantine, 1968.

Lewis, David. "An Argument for the Identity Theory," In *Philosophical Papers*, vol. 1. London: Oxford University Press, 1983.

———. "Survival and Identity," In *Philosophical Papers*, vol. 1. London: Oxford University Press, 1983.

Louch, A. R. *Explanation and Human Action*. Berkeley: University of California Press, 1966.

Lucas, John. *The Freedom of the Will*. Oxford: Clarendon, 1970.

Malcolm, Norman. *Memory and Mind*. Ithica, N.Y.: Cornell University Press, 1977.

Margolis, Joseph. *Psychotherapy and Morality*. New York: Random House, 1966.

Matson, W. I. "Why Isn't the Mind-Body Problem Ancient?" In *Mind, Matter and Method*, ed P. K. Feyerabend and Grover Maxwell. Minneapolis:

University of Minnesota Press, 1966.

May, Rollo. *Love and Will*. New York: Norton Press, 1961.

Melden, Abraham. *Free Action*. New York: Humanities Press, 1961.

Mill, John Stuart. *An Examination of Sir William Hamilton's Philosophy*. Reprinted in *Free Will and Determinism*, ed. Bernard Berofsky. New York: Harper and Row, 1966.

Minsky, Marvin. ed. *Semantic Information Processing*. Cambridge, Mass.: M. I. T. Press, 1968.

Nagel, Thomas. *Mortal Questions*. Cambridge, Eng.: Cambridge University Press, 1979.

———. "Physicalism," *Philosophical Review* 74 (1965).

———. *The View from Nowhere*. London: Oxford University Press, 1986.

———. *What Does It All Mean?* London: Oxford University Press, 1987.

The New American Bible. Washington, D.C.: Catholic University Press, 1970.

Oesterley, W. O. E. *The Gospel Parables in the Light of Their Jewish Background*. New York: Macmillan, 1936.

Parfit, Derek. *Reasons and Persons*. London: Oxford University Press, 1984.

Peters, Richard. *The Concept of Motivation*. New York: Humanities Press, 1968.

Plato. *Phaedo*, trans. H. Trendennick, In *Collected Dialogues*, ed. E. Hamilton and D. Cairns. Princeton, N.J.: Princeton University Press, 1961.

Putnam, Hilary. "Minds and Machines" In *Dimensions of the Mind*, ed. Sidney Hook. New York: Colliers, 1961.

Reid, Thomas. *Essay on the Active Powers of the Mind*. In Works, ed. J. Dugal. Charleston: Etheridge, 1813.

Rieff, Philip. *Freud: The Mind of the Moralist*. New York: Anchor, 1961.

Rorty, Richard. "Mind-Body, Privacy and Catagories," *Review of Metaphysics* 19 (1965).

———. *Philosophy and the Mirror of Nature*. Princeton, N.J.: Princeton University Press, 1979.

Ryle, Gilbert. *The Concept of Mind*. New York: Barnes and Noble. 1949.

Sankowski, Edward. "Freedom, Determinism and Character," *Mind* 889 (1980).

Sartre, Jean-Paul. *Being and Nothingness: An Essay on Phenomenological Ontology*, trans. Hazel E. Barnes. New York: Pocket Books, 1966.

Sayre, Kenneth. *Consciousness: A Philosophic Study of Minds and Machines*. New York: Random House, 1969.

Schafer, Roy. "Action: Its Place in Psychoanalytic Interpretation and Theory," In *Annual of Psychoanalysis* 1 (1973).

Searle, John. *Intentionality*. Cambridge, Eng.: Cambridge University Press, 1983.

Shaffer, Jerome. "Mental Events and the Brain," *Journal of Philosophy* 60 (1963).

Smart, John J. C. *Philosophy and Scientific Realism*. New York: Humanities Press, 1963.

———. "Sensations and Brain Processes" *Philosophical Review* 67 (1959).

———. *Utilitarianism: For and Against*. Cambridge, Eng.: Cambridge University Press, 1973.

Spinoza, Baruch. *Ethics*, trans. R. Elwes. New York: Dover, 1955.

Strawson, Galen. *Freedom and Belief*. Oxford: Clarendon, 1986.

Strawson, P. F. "Freedom and Resentment." In *Philosophy of Thought and Action*. London: Oxford University Press, 1968.

Szasz, Thomas. *The Ethics of Psychoanalysis*. New York: Basic Books, 1965.

———. *The Manufacture of Madness*. New York: Harper, 1970.

———. *The Myth of Mental Illness*. New York: Hoeber-Harper, 1961.

Thornberg, H. D. ed. *Contemporary Adolescence*. Belmont, Calf.: Wadsworth, 1971.

Trent, R. D. *Notes on the Parables of Our Lord*. New York: Appleton, 1880.

Van den Berg, J. H. *A Different Existence*. Pittsburgh: Duquesne University Press, 1972.

Van Inwagen. Peter. *Essay on Free Will*. Oxford: Clarendon, 1983.

Watson, Gary. "Free Agency," *Journal of Philosophy* 83 (1986).

Bibliography

Weizenbaum, Joseph. *Computer Power and Human Reason.* San Francisco: Freeman, 1976.

Wiggins, David. "Towards a Reasonable Libertarianism," In *Essays on Freedom of Action,* ed. T. Honderich. London: Routeledge and Kegan Paul, 1973.

Wiggins, J., And Schoeck, E., eds. *Psychiatry and Responsibility.* Princeton, N. J.: Van Nostrand, 1960.

Williams, B. A. O. "Moral Luck," *Proceedings of the Aristotelian Society,* supp. vol. 50 (1976).

Winch, Peter. *The Idea of a Social Science.* London: Routledge and Kegan Paul, 1958.

INDEX

Index

Index

Index